101 THINGS TO DO IN KEY WEST

Gary J. Sikorski

KHOLISA

Schiffer
Publishing Ltd

4880 Lower Valley Road • Atglen, PA 19310

Other Schiffer Books by the Author:

101 Things to Do in Martha's Vineyard,
978-0-7643-4953-9
101 Things to Do in Rhode Island,
978-0-7643-5138-9

Other Schiffer Books on Related Subjects:

Miami at Night, Bill Brothers,
978-0-7643-5028-3
Miami, Real and Imagined, Hank Klein,
978-0-7643-5175-4

Photos courtesy of Nomadic SUP

Designed by Brenda McCallum

Type set in Cinzel/Times

ISBN: 978-0-7643-5476-2
Printed in China

Published by Schiffer Publishing, Ltd.
4880 Lower Valley Road
Atglen, PA 19310
Phone: (610) 593-1777; Fax: (610) 593-2002
E-mail: Info@schifferbooks.com
Web: www.schifferbooks.com

For our complete selection of fine books on this and related subjects, please visit www.schifferbooks.com. You may also write for a free catalog.

Schiffer Publishing's titles are available at special discounts for bulk purchases for sales promotions or premiums. Special editions, including personalized covers, corporate imprints, and excerpts, can be created in large quantities for special needs. For more information, contact the publisher.

We are always looking for people to write books on new and related subjects. If you have an idea for a book, please contact us at proposals@schifferbooks.com.

CONTENTS

PREFACE | 4

ACKNOWLEDGMENTS | 6

INTRODUCTION | 8

A PERFECT DAY ON KEY WEST | 13

MAP OF KEY WEST | 14

101 THINGS TO DO | 16

101 THINGS TO DO (in a handy list) | 144

INDEX | 150

PREFACE

I am thrilled to say that this is my third book in a wonderful series of photographic travel guides, and each has been a real joy to create. Whereas my first project focused on Martha's Vineyard and the second on Rhode Island, this guide now brings you the excitement of the little tropical paradise island that is very dear to my heart. I've been so lucky to have been able to experience Key West over the last four decades; first as a visitor who came to bathe in its sunshine and soak in the nightlife, and then as a resident who came to work in the hospitality industry to support my nomadic lifestyle. I've seen the island grow and develop over these decades; from the heady days before the cruise ships arrived, when shrimp boats were the only crafts in the harbor and the only crowds were found waiting in line to get inside the legendary Monster Disco, to the current days of full-scale renovations that have brought an influx of national chain stores and clubs. And although commercialization has managed to rear its head on the island, you can still find those charming, authentic Old Town haunts and still feel the same peaceful tranquility of days-gone-by.

I had a wonderful time visiting my old stopping grounds to compile, photograph, and complete this work of which I am so proud. The locally caught seafood was just as fresh and delectable as I remember. The old wooden Conch-style houses were just as charming, and the aqua-blue waters that surround the island just as vast. But it was, once again, the people of Key West, with their joyous carefree outlook on life, that were the highlight of my return. The artists and writers, chefs and bartenders, hair-stylists and old hippies have ventured from near and far to make Key West their home. It was so nice spending time with all of you! I hope everyone will have as much fun with my 101 suggestions of things to do as I have had bringing them to you.

ACKNOWLEDGMENTS

6

It was such a joy returning to Key West to create this guide. It would not have been possible to give life to this book without the assistance of so many friends, old and new, that helped me in some way along my journey. To all of you, I am so very grateful.

First, for their kind generosity, contributive information, and for providing some of their fantastic photography, I'd like to thank Rich Welter, Laura McKenna, Piper Smith, Syd Kerr, Jess at Hindu Charters, Adele Williams, Matt Harris, Gary Yahoo, Dave Gonzales, Alex Appel, Captain Seth Salzmann, Paul Menta, Crystal Villegas, Cody White, Jeff Johnson, Larry Blackbum, Rod and Mary Veal, Mitch Hollingsworth, Graff Kelly, and Eliza Warren and Chic (who were especially nice, extra cookies for you two!).

Secondly, I would be remiss if I did not thank Jonathan Gross at the Rooftop Café for his helpful suggestions and wonderful hospitality, and I could not have completed my work without the kindness of Claudia Vandenabeele at the Southwinds Motel and Jeff Smead at the Island House Resort. The help, advice, and assistance all of you provided was heartfelt and very much appreciated.

I am also very grateful to Jim Gale of the Monroe County Property Appraisers Office for providing the maps found in this book. I'd also like to express my gratefulness and sincere thanks to Judy Courtemanche for her help reviewing and proofreading my text. Your expertise was invaluable.

Lastly, a hearty handshake and many thanks to my editor-extraordinaire, Jesse Marth. Once again, you and everyone at Schiffer Publishing have been such a pleasure to work with. As always, I am so pleased with the wonderful results of all your hard work.

Thank you all very, very much.

INTRODUCTION

As the song goes, "Don't worry 'bout a thing, 'cause every little thing, gonna be alright." And such is the sentiment on the tropical paradise island of Key West, the last little tiny isle on a series of peninsulas that stretch 120 miles south from the northernmost isle of Key Largo. Often referred to as the "first island of the Caribbean," this two-by-four-mile plot of paradise is actually closer to Cuba than it is to Miami. Now would be the perfect time to visit and let *101 Things to Do in Key West* guide you on your adventure. Get ready to party in the infamous bars along Duval Street, search for sharks and dolphins out on the beautiful Atlantic Ocean, bike along colorful village streets and hidden alleys, kayak through the exotic mangroves, enjoy a fresh coconut picked right off the tree, and stretch out on an exotic oceanfront beach. So squeeze an extra lime in your margarita—let's explore Key West!

The island of Key West has always been a very welcoming place, and this hospitable attitude can be traced all the way back to the original Native American population who were initially friendly to the first white explorers they encountered. When the Spanish conquistadors, who used the flow of the Gulf Stream to help them sail back and forth to Europe with their spoils, finally stopped on the island and went ashore, what they found—in addition to a friendly welcome—was a shoreline that was littered with the bleached bones of the indigenous population. So they called the place *Cayo Hueso*, meaning "island of bones." Subsequent Bahamian settlers pronounced this Spanish name as "Key West," and that's the name that has remained to this day.

By the 1820s, Key West started to flourish thanks to many sea-driven enterprises. Ships sailing to and from Havana filled their vessels with fish, sea turtles, and sponges, and Key West became a designated port of entry for these boats. But the Gulf Stream routes that were used by the ships transporting goods were also the same traveling routes used by treasure-laden vessels sailing back to Europe. These passing boats inspired piracy, and soon this precarious route was consumed with pirates lurking between channels waiting to raid the ships' cargoes of gold and silver. When the United States gained possession of the Florida Keys in 1821, the island took on a strategic naval importance and also became the base of operations to fight the piracy that was raging in the nearby Gulf of Mexico. Commander David Porter was called upon by the Navy in 1830 to put an end to the troublesome piracy. Porter and his crew were able to overtake the bandits, and the Navy has had a huge presence on the island ever since.

The wrecking industry was next to dramatically influence the island. Many of the trading vessels that sailed the seas often ran aground on the treacherous reefs, and their precious cargo would spill into the sea. The wreckers were the men who raced to recover the payload from the ocean floor. The competition to reach the lost freight became so fierce that a licensing system was created for the wreckers. By 1860, mainly because of the fortunes being made by salvaging millions of dollars of cargo from local shipwrecks, Key West was on its way to becoming one of the richest cities in Florida.

After the Cuban Revolution of 1868 the era of cigar manufacturing began. Señor Vicente Martinez Ybor moved his cigar-making factory to Key West from Havana. The E. H. Gato cigar factory soon followed, as did over two dozen other similar factories, making Key West the cigar manufacturing capital of the United States. The industry employed more than 10,000 Cubans and flourished on the island until 1890, when the city of Tampa offered lower taxes to entice the manufacturers to move their businesses to Ybor City. The factories did move, but many of the Cubans stayed and their influence in music, cuisine, and art has endured on the island to this day.

The southernmost isle of Key West was rather isolated up to this point in time, really only accessible by sea. But all this changed in 1912, when oil tycoon Henry Flagler connected Key West to the mainland with the completion of the Florida East Coast Railway. Once considered a foolish and impossible dream, Flagler's Overseas Railway helped to make Key West one of America's largest deepwater ports, which led to increased trade with the Caribbean. Unfortunately, a massive hurricane ravaged the Upper and Middle Keys in

1935, destroying much of Flagler's Railway. When you make the drive to Key West today you'll see parts of the overseas track that have been repurposed as fishing piers. The route to Key West that replaced the railway was a series of bridges that connected the islands. Overtime, those bridges have been overhauled and rebuilt to form the Overseas Highway, which is now an extension of U.S. Highway 1, the main route of access onto the island.

By the way, ever wonder why Key West is referred to as the Conch Republic? Here's the reason. In 1982, the United States Border Patrol set up a checkpoint on U.S. 1 at the Last Chance Saloon in Florida City. The Border Patrol stopped every car leaving the Keys, supposedly searching for drug smugglers and illegal immigrants attempting to enter the mainland. The blockade produced seventeen miles of traffic jams, which greatly paralyzed the Keys and crippled the flow of tourism. The mayor of Key West sought an injunction to stop the roadblock, which would have alleviated the traffic problem. But when the injunction was refused the mayor announced to TV crews that afternoon, "Tomorrow at noon Key West will secede from the Union!" The next day the Conch Republic was formed and the mayor was proclaimed Prime Minister of the Republic. He immediately declared war on the United States. After one minute at war the Republic surrendered, and applied for one billion dollars in foreign aid and war relief to rebuild! You will still see the bright blue flag with the Conch Republic emblem and motto, "We seceded where others have failed" flying all over Key West.

Today, in good part due to the ease of reaching the island via that same Overseas Highway, Key West is being visited by more people than in any other time in its history. Not surprisingly, tourism has become the main industry on the isle. And although this southernmost destination at the end of U.S. 1 is heavily visited, it still remains remote, unique, and tropically sensual. Just as it was decades ago, it is still a haven for artists and writers, street performers and musicians, treasure hunters and bartenders. That unmistakable sound of mopeds weaving through the colorful village streets still gives way to the pleasant melody of street musicians and the crowing of the Key West gypsy chickens that roam freely everywhere on the island. The wonderful aroma of freshly ground espresso beans still mixes with the distinctive smell of hand-rolled Cuban leaf cigars. Happy hour still blends into dinner. And everything is still overshadowed by that magnificent, world-famous Key West sunset.

101 Things to Do in Key West is about to take you on an exciting photographic journey. We'll guide you down hidden lanes and along sandy beaches where you will discover not only the most well-known sightseeing destinations and activities, but also the places where you're most likely to find the locals hanging out. You are probably going to find many exciting adventures you might not have known existed, even if you live here! We've also included many interesting tips and helpful suggestions that will aid you in making the most of your visit. So, fill your plastic cup with your favorite beverage (open containers are legal here!), put on your favorite pair of sandals, and begin your excursion into the best ways to enjoy this tropical paradise. You're about to climb aboard a historic wooden schooner for an elegant morning mimosa as you sail out over the Atlantic, discover colorful works of art created by local artisans, get wise to the best places to enjoy authentic Cuban cuisine, rejuvenate your body with an unforgettable total-body massage right on the beach, and experience all the live entertainment on Mallory Square as the screaming orange sun fades over the horizon at the world-famous Key West Sunset Celebration.

Turn the page, and let's go visit Key West!

A PERFECT DAY ON
KEY WEST

I know most of you would love to experience all of my 101 things to do, but a lengthy stay might not be in your cards. Because of its close proximity to Miami and many other Keys, the southernmost island paradise is, for some, just a one-day excursion.

Many times I've been asked by these folks, "I'm only going down to Key West for the day, what should I do?" Realizing it would be very difficult, not to mention impossible, to do all of my 101 things in one day, I've created a manageable itinerary for all you day-trippers. So here are my suggestions for that perfect day in beautiful Key West.

8:00 a.m.	Start your day off with a nice breakfast and a Cuban coffee at historic Pepe's Café. This local favorite in Old Town has been serving signature dishes since 1909.
9:00 a.m.	Time for a little sightseeing. Arrive early and have your picture taken next to the Southernmost Point. Explore the Butterfly Conservatory. Climb to the top of the lighthouse, then walk across the street and visit the Hemingway House. Buy a coconut from the street vendor and enjoy some fresh coconut water!
12:00 p.m.	Head over to Banana Bay Marina and get out on the water on a spectacular Dolphin Safari Charter. Don't forget your towel, because you will also be going snorkeling on this trip.
4:00 p.m.	Return to dry land and venture over to the Schooner Wharf Bar. Enjoy a cold beer, a bite to eat, live music, and watch the sailboats coming and going.
5:30 p.m.	You're already at the historic Seaport, so take a stroll along the Harbor Walk. Check out all the tall ships and watch the return of the deep-sea fishing charters.
6:00 p.m.	Mallory Square is close by, and most of the crowds are heading that way. Spend a little time in the plaza shopping for affordable souvenirs, then cross the street to Agave 308 for a handcrafted tequila cocktail.
7:00 p.m.	You can't miss it . . . Key West's world-famous Sunset Celebration on Mallory Square. Arrive early to watch all the entertaining acts before the sun goes down.
8:00 p.m.	Time for some fresh local seafood! Right across the street from Mallory Square is where you'll find the tropical Rooftop Café. Grab a table along the rail on the second floor and prepare yourself for an unforgettable dinner.
10:00 p.m.	Cap off your memorable day with a walk down lively Duval Street. The sidewalk will be full of festive people bouncing from bar to bar. Be sure to stop at the legendary Sloppy Joe's Bar to listen to one of their great live bands.
1:00 a.m.	Realize that you just had too much fun today and you are probably too tired for the drive north. Jump into a pedicab and head over to the Southwinds Motel and spend the night! Sweet Dreams!

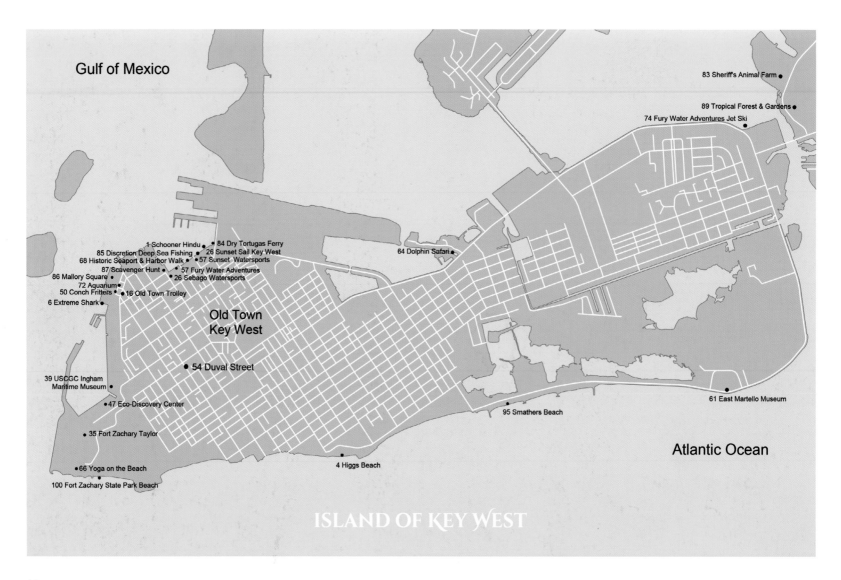

Gulf of Mexico

83 Sheriff's Animal Farm ●

89 Tropical Forest & Gardens ●

74 Fury Water Adventures Jet Ski

1 Schooner Hindu
● 84 Dry Tortugas Ferry
85 Discretion Deep Sea Fishing ● 26 Sunset Sail Key West
68 Historic Seaport & Harbor Walk ● ● 57 Sunset Watersports
87 Scavenger Hunt ● 57 Fury Water Adventures
86 Mallory Square ● ● 26 Sebago Watersports
72 Aquarium ●
50 Conch Fritters ● ● 16 Old Town Trolley
6 Extreme Shark ●

64 Dolphin Safari ●

Old Town
Key West

● 54 Duval Street

39 USCGC Ingham
Maritime Museum ●

● 47 Eco-Discovery Center

● 35 Fort Zachary Taylor

61 East Martello Museum ●

95 Smathers Beach

Atlantic Ocean

● 66 Yoga on the Beach
100 Fort Zachary State Park Beach ●

4 Higgs Beach

ISLAND OF KEY WEST

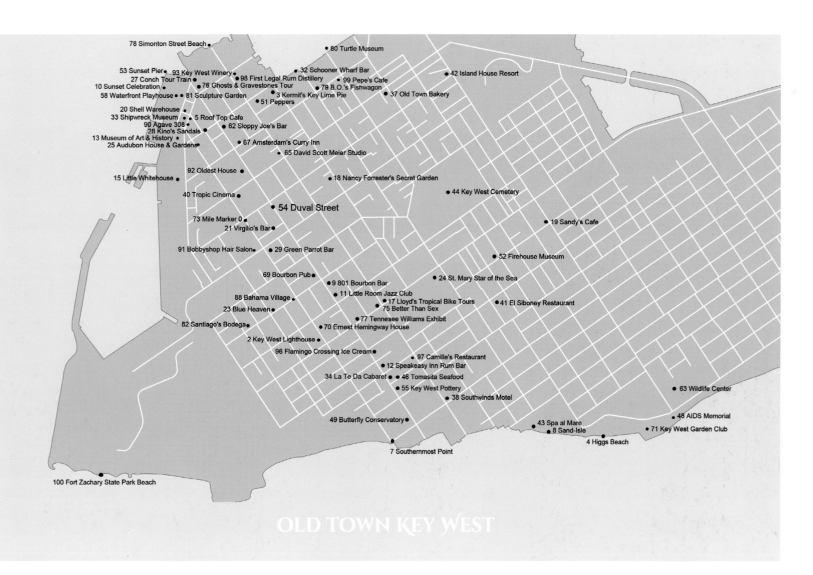

78 Simonton Street Beach   80 Turtle Museum

53 Sunset Pier   93 Key West Winery   32 Schooner Wharf Bar   42 Island House Resort
27 Conch Tour Train   98 First Legal Rum Distillery   99 Pepe's Cafe
10 Sunset Celebration   76 Ghosts & Gravestones Tour   79 B.O.'s Fishwagon   37 Old Town Bakery
58 Waterfront Playhouse   81 Sculpture Garden   3 Kermit's Key Lime Pie
20 Shell Warehouse   51 Peppers
33 Shipwreck Museum   5 Roof Top Cafe
90 Agave 308   62 Sloppy Joe's Bar
28 Kino's Sandals
13 Museum of Art & History
25 Audubon House & Gardens   67 Amsterdam's Curry Inn
65 David Scott Meier Studio

92 Oldest House
15 Little Whitehouse   18 Nancy Forrester's Secret Garden

40 Tropic Cinema   44 Key West Cemetery

54 Duval Street

73 Mile Marker 0   19 Sandy's Cafe
21 Virgilio's Bar

91 Bobbyshop Hair Salon   29 Green Parrot Bar

52 Firehouse Museum

69 Bourbon Pub   24 St. Mary Star of the Sea
9 801 Bourbon Bar
88 Bahama Village   11 Little Room Jazz Club
17 Lloyd's Tropical Bike Tours   41 El Siboney Restaurant
23 Blue Heaven   75 Better Than Sex
82 Santiago's Bodega   77 Tennessee Williams Exhibit
70 Ernest Hemingway House
2 Key West Lighthouse
96 Flamingo Crossing Ice Cream   97 Camille's Restaurant
12 Speakeasy Inn Rum Bar
34 La Te Da Cabaret   46 Tomasita Seafood
55 Key West Pottery   63 Wildlife Center
38 Southwinds Motel
48 AIDS Memorial
49 Butterfly Conservatory   43 Spa al Mare
8 Sand-Isle   71 Key West Garden Club
4 Higgs Beach
7 Southernmost Point

100 Fort Zachary State Park Beach

OLD TOWN KEY WEST

15

No. 1

Start your day with an elegant Morning Mimosa Sail aboard the Schooner *Hindu*

Schooner *Hindu*
Key West Bight Marina | 0 Margaret Street | www.sailschoonerhindu.com

You may never get the opportunity to ride in a historic, spectacularly appointed, wooden schooner like this again—so you better jump aboard while you're here! This majestic tall ship was built in 1925 and has been exquisitely restored; and with the motor off and her massive sails catching the wind, the ride is breathtaking. Their peaceful and relaxing Morning Mimosa Cruise, which includes locally made pastries, freshly brewed Cuban coffee, bottomless mimosas, and priceless memories, just might be the highlight of your vacation. The elegant schooner and her extremely friendly crew also offer a popular sunset sail, but put the morning mimosa cruise at the top of your "must-do" list.

No. 2

Climb to the top of the Key West Lighthouse for a panoramic view of the city

Key West Lighthouse
938 Whitehead Street | www.kwahs.org/museums/lighthouse-keepers-quarters/history

A spectacular view of Key West and the Atlantic Ocean awaits you atop the Key West Lighthouse, as long as you don't have vertigo! You'll need to climb eighty-eight steps up a small spiral staircase to the viewing platform, but the winding trek is worth it. If you find yourself a huffin' and a puffin' on the way up, just remember, it's a lot easier on the way down. Afterwards, don't miss the small museum inside the former lighthouse keeper's quarters, where you can explore the belongings and photographs of the former lighthouse occupants. The lighthouse complex is located just a stone's throw from the world-famous Hemingway House on Whitehead Street.

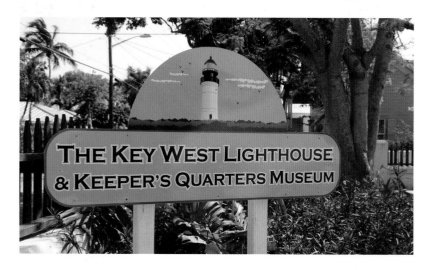

No. 3

Indulge in a little slice of paradise at the original Kermit's Key West Key Lime Pie Shoppe

Kermit's Key West Key Lime Pie Shoppe
200 Elizabeth Street | www.keylimeshop.com

Key limes just don't seem to travel well—so for real, authentic, tart Key lime flavor, you absolutely must have a slice of Key lime pie while you're here. And the best pie on the island is found at the famous yellow and green shop on the corner of Elizabeth and Greene Streets. Kermit's has mastered everything that's Key lime, including cookies, salsa, chutney, taffy, jelly beans, olive oil, soaps, shampoos, and of course, Key lime pie!

TIP: The *piece de resistance* is their chocolate covered Key lime pie on a stick.

No. 4

Join the locals in a spirited game of beach volleyball at Higgs Beach

Volleyball at Higgs Beach
Atlantic Avenue (near Salute! Restaurant)

The Clarence S. Higgs Memorial Beach, adjacent to the Waldorf Astoria's Casa Marina, is one of the more inviting beaches because of its diverse array of activities and offerings. It features two very popular volleyball courts, usually busy with friendly young locals who don't mind letting others share in the fun. Just ask! And, if you get tired of sunning or wading in the shallow water, you can explore the African Burial Grounds, Salute's beachfront restaurant, the AIDS Memorial, a historic Civil War-era fort, and the Key West Garden Club—all right along the beach!

TIP: If you would like to go swimming, walk all the way down the little pier on the far right and use the stairs to get into the waist-deep water.

No. 5

Dine above the streets and beneath the stars at the Roof Top Café, a local favorite!

Roof Top Cafe
308 Front Street | www.rooftopcafekeywest.com

Aptly named as it sits above the storefronts along the stretch of Front Street that faces Mallory Square, the popular Roof Top Café is one of the preeminent "island-casual" dining establishments in the Conch Republic. Owned by restaurateurs Norman and Wednesday Vogel, and superbly managed by Jonathan Gross and celebrated Executive Chef Brendan Orr, the award-winning restaurant has been a Key West landmark for more than thirty years. You can choose to enjoy their sensational island cuisine either inside the airy dining room with vaulted wood-beamed ceilings surrounded by tropical foliage, or on the delightful second-floor balcony under the canopy of a magnificent Chinese mahogany tree. Either way it will be a dining experience you won't soon forget!

Roof Top Café
The Cuisine of Executive Chef Brendan Orr

Chef Orr (bottom left) has been creating culinary wonders at the Roof Top since 2004. Celebrated as one of the finest chefs in South Florida, he is renowned for his unique "New-Island" cuisine, which combines local ingredients with tropical fruits, spices from the Far East, and staples from the Mediterranean. Dishes like lobster gnocchi with black truffle cream sauce, grilled mahi-mahi with a mango salsa and citrus beurre blanc, coconut-encrusted sea scallops served with basmati rice, and an unbelievable seafood bouillabaisse are some of the popular choices found on Chef Orr's delectable menu.

Special of the Night!

You can always count on the scrumptious dishes on the Roof Top's menu being prepared to perfection. But you might want to pass on the standard favorites because Chef Orr's nightly specials are going to be hard to resist. Appetizers like kombu-cured yellowfin tuna with spicy soy caramel (below); wakame salad and micro radish greens; and entrees like locally caught hogfish (top left) with herb oil, tomato jam, and crab mashed potatoes are a few of the sensational creations you might encounter on any given night.

No. 6

Get an up close look at the sharks with Key West Extreme Adventures Shark Tours

Extreme Adventures Shark Tours
245 Front Street | www.kwextremeadventures.com

What a fantastic adventure! To tell you the truth, I was hoping to see *a* shark on this tour. Wow, it was shark after shark after shark. The friendly and extremely knowledgeable Captain Harris, who has more than thirty years of guiding experience, and his first mate Clay knew where to find the action. The exciting two-hour cruise on their comfortable, thirty-four foot "Tiger Cat" catamaran was enhanced by sightings of sea turtles, stingrays, and wild dolphins. And the information about sharks, marine animals, the environment, and conservation was invaluable. Don't miss this trip!

No. 7

Have your photo taken standing next to the colorful buoy at the Southernmost Point

Southernmost Point
Corner of Whitehead and South Streets | www.southernmostpointwebcam.com

The most iconic attraction in Key West is undoubtedly the world-famous red, black, and gold cement buoy that designates the southernmost point in the continental United States (Hawaii is actually 400 miles further south). The massive buoy attracts visitors from around the world, so you'll need to wait patiently in the long line to capture the moment you stood closer to Cuba than anyone else in the country. Smile for the camera!

No. 8

Head over to Sand-Isle and take a professionally taught sand sculpting class

Sand-Isle Sand Sculptures
1500 Reynolds Street | www.sandisle.com/sand-sculpting-101

Sand-Isle bills itself as being the makers of the "coolest sand sculptures on planet earth," and after walking by the unbelievable works of art that line the beach behind the Casa Marina, I'd have to agree! Marianne and Chris, the husband and wife team that started Sand-Isle, have quite a reputation for creating imaginative and remarkable sand sculptures all around the world. Treat yourself to their two-and-a-half-hour workshop and learn the techniques that have helped them construct extraordinary sand creations for major corporations, international competitions, and popular television shows. Yeah, really cool!

No. 9

Win some really wild prizes at the multi-decade island tradition of Drag Queen Bingo

Drag Queen Bingo @ 801 Bourbon Bar
801 Duval Street | www.801bourbon.com

This is definitely not your grandma's bingo! The hugely entertaining weekly affair has been an island tradition for more than thirty years. Hosted by the legendary Q Mitch, you can expect raunchy humor, funny sing-a-longs, and lots of sexual innuendos. It's a blast, and all the proceeds lovingly go to local charities. If you are in Key West on a Sunday, you might miss church, but do not miss Drag Queen Bingo!

No. 10

Join the crowds on Mallory Dock for the nightly Sunset Celebration

Sunset Celebration
Mallory Square | www.sunsetcelebration.org

If you come to Key West, you are sure to eventually end up on the dock at Mallory Square for Key West's world-famous Sunset Celebration. You'll marvel at the spectacular pink, orange, yellow, and red colors as the sun sinks into the Gulf of Mexico, but you will also be immersed in the amazing carnival atmosphere. Visitors from around the world find themselves taking part in the jugglers, magicians, fire-eaters, tightrope-walkers, psychics, artists, local musicians, food vendors, and the sheer excitement that has captivated the crowds on Mallory Dock for decades.

TIP: To enjoy all that Sunset Celebration has to offer (and to claim a spot for the best view of the sunset) plan to arrive at least an hour before the sun goes down.

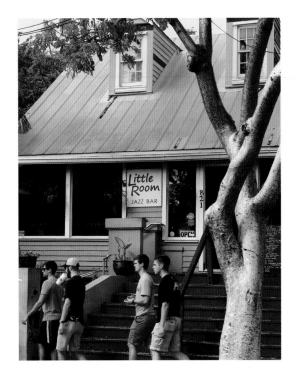

No. 11

Combine a sophisticated drink with some great tunes at the Little Room Jazz Club

Little Room Jazz Club
821 Duval Street | www.littleroomjazzclub.com

The posh, intimate Little Room Jazz Club is a refreshing change from the raucous music scene typically found just a short distance away down Duval Street. It's also a bit more upscale, so you'd probably be more comfortable in a button-down, rather than a t-shirt. The venue has an outstanding wine selection, and features exciting live ensembles playing jazz, blues, soul, and swing seven nights a week. If you're lucky, you might even hear a few Cuban gems!

TIP: There's some great elevated outdoor seating in front of the club that's perfect for drinking and people watching.

No. 12

Warm your spirit with a selection of fine rums at the historic Speakeasy Inn Rum Bar

The Rum Bar
1117 Duval Street | www.speakeasyinn.com

This wonderfully quaint little bar is found on the ground floor of the Speakeasy Inn. It's in a building that was the former home of Raul Vaquez, a nineteenth-century cigar selector whose true passion was rum running between Key West and Cuba. The former prohibition-era speakeasy has a nice comfortable local feel to it, a place where the conversation is more important than the music. The shelves are stacked with more than 230 bottles of premium rums, which complement an excellent list of specialty rum drinks. Their wraparound front porch is a great spot to spend a lazy afternoon in paradise!

No. 13

Discover splendid local artwork and historical artifacts at the Key West Museum of Art & History

Key West Museum of Art & History
281 Front Street | www.kwahs.org

A wonderful collection specifically focusing on the island and assembled by the Key West Art & Historical Society can be found inside the historic four-story Custom House, an architectural marvel that originally housed the island's customs office, postal service, and district courts. The seven galleries found throughout the imposing building feature exhibits recalling when the island was first settled, the establishment of the Flagler Overseas Railway, WWII memorabilia, a salute to Ernest Hemingway, along with plenty of local artwork and interesting island artifacts. Some very cool and interesting sculptures surround the building, so make sure you walk around the exterior of the museum.

No. 14

Get a load of all the colorfully dressed characters masquerading around the island!

The Colorful People of Key West
Everywhere along Duval Street!

You don't need a festival or special event to get dressed up in a flamboyant costume on this paradise island! On any given day you're bound to witness a parade of gaudy characters carousing up and down the mile-long Duval Street. Swingers, drag queens, bikers, and just plain ol' regular folks dressed in splashy outfits adorned with beads, flowers, masks, rainbow colors, and feathers are part of the reason for Key West's undeniable "carefree" reputation. Grab a wig, a beer, and some body paint . . . and join in on the fun!

NO. 15

Experience a historic presidential winter retreat at the Harry S. Truman Little White House

Harry S. Truman Little White House
111 Front Street | www.trumanlittlewhitehouse.com

Located in the Truman Annex neighborhood of Old Town, the Little White House was the vacation home and winter White House of President Harry S. Truman, who spent 175 days of his presidency here from 1946 through 1952. Six other former presidents have also visited here for rest and relaxation, including Bill Clinton in 2005 and Jimmy Carter in 2007. The impressive grounds are free to roam, but do buy a ticket for the forty-five minute guided tour. It's wonderfully interesting and very informative.

TIP: You can save some bucks by purchasing a Little White House/Hemingway House combination ticket.

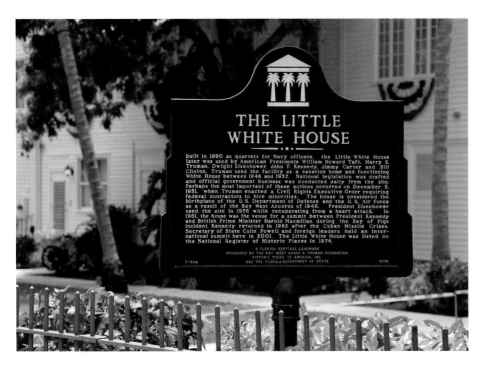

No. 16

Jump on the Old Town Trolley and be treated to a narrated tour of the island

Old Town Trolley Tours
1 Whitehead Street | www.trolleytours.com/key-west

If you will be in Key West for just a short period of time and want to see the whole shebang, then jump aboard the friendly orange and green Old Town Trolley. The informative and sometimes humorous tour covers a lot of ground, and eventually passes virtually every major sightseeing attraction on the island. There are thirteen stops along the winding route, and you can hop off at any point, explore the area, and then hop back on the next time another trolley passes.

TIP: Your ticket is valid for the entire day, so long breaks are totally cool.
(Personally, I suggest a midafternoon cocktail stop. Lighten up, you're on vacation!)

No. 17

Peddle through hidden back streets and sample local fruits on Lloyd's Tropical Bike Tour

Lloyd's Tropical Bike Tour
601 Truman Avenue | www.lloydstropicalbiketour.com

What a great way to see the real Key West! Lloyd is friendly and personable, and he's been leading this wonderful tropical bike tour for more than twenty-four years. The pace is very leisurely, down quaint streets and hidden lanes, with many stops along the way. You'll see classic Bahamian and Conch-style houses, visit botanical gardens, explore the Wildlife Center and a historic fort, and taste freshly cracked coconut and a delicious variety of local fruits, like sapodilla or Surinam cherry. The best part of the tour . . . Lloyd will leave you with a smile on your face!

NO. 18

Interact with the rescued parrots and macaws at Nancy Forrester's Secret Garden

Nancy Forrester's Secret Garden
518 Elizabeth Street | www.nancyforrester.com

Nancy Forrester is a teacher, artist, environmental activist, and a plant and animal lover who has been rescuing and rehoming orphaned parrots for more than thirty years. Her breathtaking tiny garden, filled with rare plants and dozens of large parrot cages, is a tropical rainforest paradise found behind her small two-story home on lazy, residential Elizabeth Street. The little secret garden is a gem, and Nancy is a true delight. She welcomes visitors with open arms, gladly answers questions, educates, and tells stories. But her real charm comes from the love of her parrots that radiates throughout the tranquil oasis. Do stop in . . . the parrots love to sing, hear music, meet people, and be held!

No. 19

Savor an authentic Cuban café con leche at the popular Sandy's Café

Sandy's Café
1026 White Street | www.kwsandyscafe.com

Sharing the same building with the huge neighborhood M&M Laundromat, Sandy's Café is really nothing more than a little take-out window—but this walk-up joint serves some of the best, authentic Cuban "fast-food" on the island. The popular Cuban sandwich (ham, pork, lettuce, tomato, pickles, mayo, and mustard) is absolutely delicious. And do not leave Key West until you've savored Sandy's café con leche (espresso, steamed milk, and sugar). There's only a few bar stools for seating, it's a little bit off the beaten path, and it's cash only, but Sandy's is the real deal. Don't miss it!

No. 20

Pick up some exotic seashells at the Shell Warehouse

Shell Warehouse
1 Whitehead Street, Mallory Square | 305-294-5168

Key West has miles of shoreline, but surprisingly, the selection of seashells that make their way onto the beach is virtually non-existent. So if you love things from the sea and want to take home some exotic shells, you'll need to check out the terrific selection at the Shell Warehouse. It's located in Asa Tift's nineteenth-century ice house near the Aquarium in the back of Mallory Square. The shop also has nice section of fine jewelry, local art, and plenty of decorative items for your home.

No. 21

Stumble down the alley to Virgilio's Martini Madness Monday

Virgilio's Martini Madness Monday
Down Applerouth Lane behind 524 Duval Street

If it's Monday night and you find yourself in Key West . . . you are in luck! Follow the long line of locals down Applerouth Lane to Key West's wildly popular Martini Madness Monday, one of the most anticipated drink happenings on the island. Virgilio's is housed in a cozy, open-air back room that was formerly a leather bar, and while the leather is long gone, the charming "back alley" feeling remains. Live jazz pours from the cramped stage, and five-dollar martinis pour rapid-fire from some of the island's best bartenders. The Chocolate Mint Martini, Milky Way, Key Lime Pie Martini, and Razzle Dazzle will keep you dancing well into the night!

No. 22

Travel up to Big Pine Key to get a glimpse of the miniature Key Deer

Endangered Key Deer
Big Pine Key | www.fws.gov/refuge/National_Key_Deer_Refuge

When traveling U.S. 1, either to or from Key West, you'll be passing through Big Pine Key, renowned as the home of the cute, miniature Key deer. Standing just above two feet tall, this endangered subspecies of the white-tailed deer can only be found in this area of the Florida Keys. Just drive by and you are bound to see them foraging near the roadside, especially around sunset when they are most active. Take a few minutes and detour out to the National Key Deer Refuge for a better chance of seeing the adorable animals.

TIP: DO NOT speed through Big Pine. The endangered deer frequently cross the road, which is thankfully heavily patrolled!

No. 23

Feast on creative Caribbean cuisine served in a tropical paradise at the ultra-funky Blue Heaven

Blue Heaven
729 Thomas Street | www.blueheavenkw.com

If you are looking for an authentic "Key West" dining experience, don't miss the very popular Blue Heaven restaurant that's tucked away in Bahama Village. The Floridian-Caribbean menu features some of the best food on the island, and the colorful whimsical décor is just a delight. Throw in the fact that you'll be dining aside live local bands under almond and coconut trees in a shady courtyard with cats and roosters roaming at your feet, and you got one hell of an experience. There will probably be long lines, but just belly-up to the bar or roam through the gift shop—you're in for a real treat!

No. 24

Say a little prayer amongst the architectural beauty of The Basilica of Saint Mary Star of the Sea

The Basilica of Saint Mary Star of the Sea
1010 Windsor Lane | www.stmarykeywest.com

You can't help but notice this magnificent house of worship as you drive down Truman Avenue just blocks before you reach Duval Street. The Basilica of Saint Mary Star of the Sea's welcoming portico is highlighted with beautiful rusticated walls, lunettes filled with transitional gothic arches, and two massive ninety-seven-foot towers each capped with a cross. You may recognize this beautifully landscaped church from the opening sequence of the James Bond movie *Licence to Kill*.

TIP: Follow the stone path that forms a rosary on the right side of the church and you can say a prayer in the Historic Grotto of Our Lady of Lourdes.

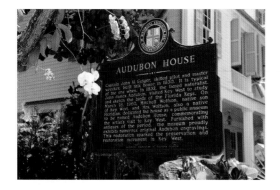

No. 25

Marvel at fragrant orchids and rare tropical palms at the Audubon House & Tropical Gardens

Audubon House & Tropical Gardens
205 Whitehead Street | www.audubonhouse.com

A nice respite from the hustle and bustle of Duval Street just a block away is the Audubon House and Gardens, which celebrates naturalist John James Audubon, the great painter and cataloguer of American birds. Along with period antiques and historical photos, twenty-eight first edition Audubon works are on display. Meander along the lush tropical garden's paved, red brick pathways and view orchids, bromeliads, an herb garden, a lovely 1840s-style nursery, and a delightful koi pond popular with the local wildlife.

No. 26

Kick back on an unforgettable sunset cruise and sail into Key West's remarkable sunset

Sunset Sail Key West
Schooner *When & If*
202 William Street | www.sunsetsailkeywest.com

This unforgettable sunset sail aboard the *When & If* really is a "highlight" experience. The beautifully restored schooner *When & If* is a legendary wooden sailing vessel built in 1939 for General George S. Patton. General Patton commented, "WHEN the war is over, AND IF I live through it, Bea and I are going to sail her around the world." Standing on her teak deck complemented by lavish bronze trim, Captain Seth's friendly crew is happy to keep the wine flowing and artisan cheese selection coming. It's a first-class sail on a first-class schooner.

Lands End Sunset Sail
Sebago Flyer **Catamaran**
205 Elizabeth Street | www.keywestsebago.com

The Lands End Sunset Sail aboard *Sebago Flyer*, a luxurious sixty-foot sailing catamaran, is another one of the great choices available for a remarkable sunset cruise. The vessel has expansive deck space and Sebago keeps the number of passengers below capacity, allowing you to move around the ship comfortably and to find a seat easily. An excellent selection of hors d'oeuvres (including peel-and-eat shrimp!), champagne, and a full bar are included in the ticket. You'll get an up close look at Mallory Square and Fort Zach, and of course, a front row seat to that world-famous Key West sunset!

Sebago's Windjammer Classic Sunset Sail
Schooner *Appledore II*
205 Elizabeth Street | www.keywestsebago.com

Take a turn at the wheel or help raise the sails aboard the Windjammer Classic Sunset Sail, another one of the fabulous sunset cruises available in Key West. Built in 1978, the famed wooden schooner *Appledore II* is a traditional two-masted tall ship. A trip aboard this eighty-six foot windjammer is a real delight. The crew is extremely personable and fresh fruit, cheeses, boutique wine, beers, and homemade sangria is offered as you peacefully head out into the Atlantic. It really is a lot of fun jockeying around this traditional nineteenth-century tall ship looking for a good viewing position as the celestial fireball sinks into the horizon.

No. 27

Climb aboard the Conch Tour Train and learn all about the history of Key West

Conch Tour Train
Front Street Depot at Mallory Square | www.conchtourtrain.com

If you arrive in Key West and you are unfamiliar with the lay of the land, one of the best ways to orient yourself is to jump on the giant choo-choo that begins at the Front Street Depot in Mallory Square. The well-narrated ninety-minute tour is kind of touristy, but the fun facts, folklore, and bits of history the conductor bellows out over the microphone are really quite interesting. It's not only a treat for little ones, but the ride is especially helpful for the elderly who might not be able to hike around the island on foot.

TIP: Make the train ride one of your first activities when you arrive. It passes most of the attractions on the island, which will help you decide what to explore later.

No. 28

Slip on a pair of handmade sandals at the world-famous Kino Sandals Factory

Kino Sandals Factory
107 Fitzpatrick Street | https://kinosandals.com

Hidden in the far corner of a tiny shopping plaza down a narrow side street near Mallory Square is where you'll find Kino Sandals, makers of some of the most comfortable, durable, and affordable sandals you might ever wear. You could pick a pair of the many different styles and colors right off of the over-stocked shelves, or sit back and watch your custom sandals being made! All Kino's sandals are handmade using natural leather uppers and natural rubber soles. They are all assembled on sewing machines located in a large factory space right behind the sales counter, using the same traditional Cuban method since 1966.

TIP: Kino Sandals make for a perfect gift or souvenir.

No. 29

Party the night away at the Green Parrot, a popular dive bar featuring great local live music

Green Parrot Bar
601 Whitehead Street | www.greenparrot.com

An institution since 1890, simply known as "The Parrot" by locals, this quintessential watering hole is regularly found on listings of the world's best dive bars. The Key West icon is as laid back as it gets. The walls are adorned with oversized portraits, unusual signs, posters, and colorful murals. The beer is cheap and the patrons are friendly. The small stage hosts incredible blues, jazz, zydeco, and rock bands. And you will usually find the dance floor overcrowded in the evening. I just love the fact that there is no glass in the window frames, keeping the place airy and tropical. It's a must-do when in Key West!

Lil' Ed & The Blues Imperials
Live at the Green Parrot Bar

The Parrot is not just known as being a great place to drink, but also as one of the best places on the island to see incredible live local and national bands. The crowds here know their music, and appreciate anything musically different—as long as it's good! The small stage has been occupied by diverse groups from Igor and the Red Elvises to Lil' Ed & The Blues Imperials. There's also a great jukebox for when the bands are on break.

No. 30

Jump on a Perfect Pedicab and be blissfully peddled to your next destination

Perfect Pedicabs | www.perfectpedicabkw.com

Key West is extremely walkable, and hiking from sight to sight (or bar to bar) is half the fun. But it could get a bit tiring in the South Florida heat. So thank God for these popular three-wheeled hooded cabs. You'll find these bike taxis virtually everywhere, especially on most street corners along Duval. Just negotiate the fare, hop on, and be blissfully chauffeured to your next destination.

TIP: Call ahead and Perfect Pedicab will pick you up at your hotel and take you on a guided tour of the island. Now that's very cool indeed.

NO. 31

Spend the day with nature paddling around the scenic mangroves

Red Mangrove Kayaking
www.redmangrovekayaking.com

Grab a paddle and join Mitch Hollingsworth on a wonderfully informative and scenically captivating kayaking trip through the calm, blue-green waters of the remote regions of the Lower Keys' back country, an area of hundreds of enchanting mangrove islands accessible only by these small boats. Mitch will guide you through a winding maze of serene canopied canals bordered by a canvas of densely tangled mangrove tree roots, and share his extensive knowledge of the vast mangrove ecosystem. You'll also have a chance at up close encounters with tropical fish, crabs, turtles, and aquatic birds foraging for food. Put this unforgettable trip on your "must-do" list!

Photos courtesy of Red Mangrove Kayaking

No. 32

Belly up to the bar at Schooner Wharf and enjoy a cold beer and great live music

Schooner Wharf Bar
202 William Street (on the harborfront) | www.schoonerwharf.com

I can actually remember when this waterfront bar was hard to find, when it wasn't near *anything*. Today, thanks to tons of development along the harbor front, the popular Schooner Wharf is near the center of the seaport action. The open-air, wonderfully timeworn local dive rightfully bills itself as "a last little piece of Old Key West." Expect to find thatched-umbrella tables filled with buckets of beer, a large oval bar plastered with colorful decals, bar stools filled with friendly locals, a great affordable menu of local seafood delicacies, and live island music coming from the small stage. This place really is a paradise found!

TIP: Wander up to the hard-to-find second-floor deck for a great view of the harbor.

NO. 33

Discover the "era of the wreckers" at the Key West Shipwreck Museum

**Key West Shipwreck
Treasure Museum
1 Whitehead Street
www.keywestshipwreck.com**

Relive the era of the wreckers, a time in the mid-1800s when the business of salvaging goods from shipwrecks made Key West the richest city per capita in the United States. The wrecker's warehouse and museum combines actors in period costumes, films, and actual recovered booty and cargo from the past to tell the story of Asa Tift. Asa was a nineteenth-century wrecker who salvaged goods off the *SS Isaac Allerton*, which was downed by a hurricane in 1856. Climb to the top of the lookout tower for a nice view of Old Town, Sunset Key, and the ocean.

NO. 34

Take in a legendary drag performance at the iconic La Te Da Cabaret

Randy Roberts Live!
La Te Da Cabaret & Piano Bar
1125 Duval Street | www.lateda.com

Come to the cabaret my friends! This intimate venue is located on the second floor of the iconic La Te Da hotel complex. Its tiny round tables, red velvet curtains, and sophisticated atmosphere make you feel as if you're at a show in Las Vegas. And the shows are absolutely fabulous! No lip-syncing here. One of my favorite headliners is the legendary Randy Roberts, whose astonishing impersonations of Cher, Bette Midler, and many others have kept him in the spotlight for more than twenty years. Expect flawless makeup, dazzling costumes, quick humor, and mesmerizing live vocals. And expect to walk away delighted and amazed!

NO. 35

Take the self-guided tour of the huge Civil War-era Fort Zachary Taylor

Fort Zachary Taylor
End of Southard Street in Truman Annex | www.floridastateparks.org/park/Fort-Taylor

Besides boasting the best beach on the island, the other reason to venture inside the fifty-four acre historic Fort Zachary Taylor State Park is the massive Civil War-era fortress known by locals as "Fort Zach." Built in the mid-1880s, the thick-walled red brick and concrete stronghold displays the largest (and extremely impressive!) collection of Civil War-era cannons in the United States. Climb up and walk around the fort's roof for a nice view of the Atlantic.

TIP: The fort does offer a guided tour once a day, but you'll have to check ahead for the time.

No. 36

Enjoy a nice hand-rolled Cuban leaf cigar

Cuban Leaf Cigars
Cigar Shops throughout the Island

There must be more cigar shops per capita in Key West than any other city in the country! And although the days of the massive cigar factories on the island are long gone, there is one thing you can still find in every cigar shop on the island: hand-rolled cigars with Cuban leaf wrappers. While there are only a few places that actually still roll their own, most shops do have an extensive classic cigar assortment along with complex "house blend" tobaccos. Grab a stogie, light 'er up, then sit back, relax, and watch the world go by!

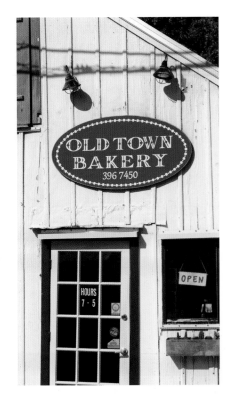

No. 37

Follow the aroma into Old Town Bakery and get your hands on their delicious sticky buns

Old Town Bakery
930 Eaton Street | www.oldtownbakerykeywest.com

Old Town Bakery is aptly named, not just because it's in Old Town, but because it has that feel of an authentic "old town" bakery. Their delicious French palmiers are light and crisp, and their flakey croissants are rich and buttery. Made-from-scratch pastries, artisan breads, cookies baked on-premises, and those unforgettable sticky buns have made Old Town Bakery a huge local favorite. The patisserie makes for a great stop if you are out on a morning bike ride or on a walk around the historic seaport.

TIP: Get there early for the best selection, as many of the pastries sell out quickly!

No. 38

Relax by one of the three outdoor pools at the affordable Southwinds Motel

Southwinds Motel
1321 Simonton Street | www.keywestsouthwinds.com

Luckily, there are still a few places in Key West where you won't have to break the bank to spend the night. At the top of that list is the quaint Southwinds Motel. This place is a gem. I've stayed in this charming motel many times in the last thirty years, and it's so well-kept and well-cared-for that you'd think it was a brand new inn! Other reasons to stay here: The staff is extremely friendly and personable, the rooms are comfortable and well-appointed, the grounds are landscaped beautifully, the motel has three pools (yes, *three* pools!), there's plenty of on-property parking (this is huge), and the location couldn't be better. Five stars in my book!

Step aboard a U.S. battleship at the USCGC *Ingham* Maritime Museum

U.S. Coast Guard Cutter *Ingham* Maritime Museum
Truman Waterfront/Southard Street | www.uscgcingham.org

Located right next to the Eco-Discovery Center on the Truman Waterfront, the massively impressive USCGC *Ingham* is the only Coast Guard battleship afloat today to receive two presidential unit citations for extraordinary heroism in action against an armed enemy. Retired from military use in 1988, after fifty-two years of service, the vessel is a time capsule of that era, with everything left on board from interesting communication equipment to old cigarette packs.

TIP: Board the ship for their sunset happy hour (with great views!) held every Friday and Saturday.

No. 40

Take in a foreign or indie film at the intimate Tropic Cinema

Tropic Cinema
416 Eaton Street | www.tropiccinema.com

Opened in 2004 after a massive renovation, this impeccably maintained art deco movie house is the pride of the Conch Republic. Rather than the big blockbuster films of the moment, the cinema wisely features documentaries, foreign, independent, and alternative movies in their intimate viewing rooms. The place is loaded with charm and character; and you can't beat a theater that offers fabulous popcorn with real butter, gourmet snacks, imported chocolates, and beer and wine! It's a great choice for those occasional rainy day blues.

No. 41

Dig into the most authentic Cuban home cooking in Florida at El Siboney Restaurant

El Siboney Restaurant
900 Catherine Street | www.elsiboneyrestaurant.com

It would be a shame to travel this close to Cuba and not experience traditional, authentic Cuban home cooking. Just step inside this off-the-beaten-path neighborhood restaurant filled with bilingual chatter and you are sure to feel as if you were in Havana. The portions here are enormous, and the food is absolutely mouth watering. High on my list are the Siboney steak, ropa vieja (shredded beef), paella valenciana for two, their sweet fried plantains, and their homemade sangria. Don't let the simple brick façade fool you; this family-run joint is a gem!

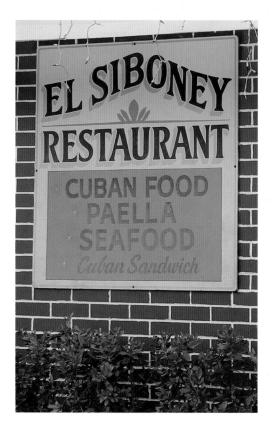

No. 42

Reserve a poolside room or just visit and join the fun at the Island House Resort

Island House Resort
1129 Fleming Street | www.islandhousekeywest.com

A resort might not be your first choice when you're deciding on where to go to grab a drink or a bite to eat, but you'll probably change your mind after visiting the fabulous Island House. This celebrated, men-only (sorry ladies) tropical paradise is often voted one of the ten best guest houses in North America. In addition to their exquisitely appointed rooms (decorated in a motif inspired by Ernest Hemingway's home in Havana) the property boasts a large heated pool, two jacuzzis, a steam room, sauna, gym, and a large sunning deck. The resort also has a tropical pool3side café that has been hailed as one of the best in Key West, and a bar that's open twenty-four hours a day. Oy Vey!

No. 43

Rejuvenate your mind, body, and spirit with a massage on the beach at Spa al Mare

Spa al Mare
1500 Reynolds Street | www.casamarinaresort.com/spa

Pass through the luxurious Waldorf Astoria's Casa Marina Resort and follow the sandy path until you see the tranquil beach cabanas surrounded by flowing white curtains and palm trees. You've found the most peaceful, relaxing plot of sand on the whole island—the private massage huts of Spa al Mare. Drift away by trying their "Ocean Breeze Indulgence," a mind- and body-altering rub-down on massage tables nestled right up at the water's edge, enhanced by the sounds of waves crashing onto the beach, palm trees swaying in the wind, gentle breezes blowing, and the scent of saltwater and essential oils in the air. Then, finish it all off with a private rinse in the outdoor bamboo shower. What a treat!

No. 44

Join the free walking tour of the aboveground vaults in historic Key West Cemetery

Key West Cemetery
701 Passover Lane | www.friendsofthekeywestcemetery.com

This might sound macabre, but this quirky, nineteen-acre cemetery located in the center of the island is quite the popular attraction. Many of the graves are in aboveground vaults, similar to the cemeteries in New Orleans. You could spend hours exploring the historic grounds, which include a Catholic section, Jewish section, the USS *Maine* plot, and the Los Martires de Cuba, which is a memorial to those who died in the 1868 Cuban Revolution.

TIP: The wide paved streets that wind throughout the property make for a nice little bike ride.

No. 45

Slip on your fins and go snorkeling in the world-famous Florida Keys Coral Reef

Havin' Fun Snorkeling
Out in the Atlantic Ocean

Want to get a personal and up close look at those colorful tropical fish? Then grab a mask, snorkel, and a pair of fins and jump into the Atlantic Ocean! Snorkeling is one of Key West's top activities, and you will find many companies offering a wide range of snorkeling adventures, from combo-packages that include snorkeling in the shallow waters of the Gulf of Mexico to the popular Florida Keys Coral Reef snorkeling adventure way out in the Atlantic. Don't worry if you're a first-timer; snorkeling is really easy to do and every trip includes a professional safety and instruction course. And most trips include free beer when the snorkeling is over!

No. 46

Buy the freshest fish on the island at Tomasita Seafood, a "secret" local favorite!

Tomasita Seafood
515 Catherine Street | 305-296-6424

Neatly hugging the sidewalk in front of a modest home in a residential neighborhood of Old Town, the tiny Tomasita Seafood stand sells fish that is about as fresh as fresh fish gets. If the sign says "open," pull the chain to ring the bell, and Tomasita comes out to the tiny screened hut. You never know what she might have on ice on any particular day. The prices can't be beat, and the more Spanish you know, the better!

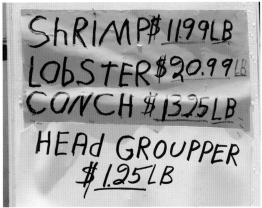

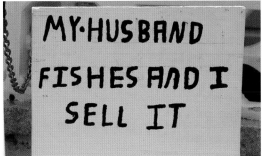

No. 47

Journey into a world of native plants and animals at the Florida Keys Eco-Discovery Center

Florida Keys Eco-Discovery Center
35 East Quay Road | http://floridakeys.noaa.gov/eco_discovery.html

The Eco-Discovery Center, with more than 6,400 square feet of exhibits and a seventy-four-seat movie theater, really is an entertaining way to learn about the natural wonders and ecosystem of the Florida Keys. The facility has lots of interactive displays highlighting conservation efforts in South Florida, interesting touchscreen computers so you can learn about habitats and coral reefs, a walk-through version of the Aquarius underwater laboratory, and a 2,500-gallon living reef tank with corals and tropical fish.

No. 48

Pay tribute to those who have died of AIDS at the Key West AIDS Memorial

Key West AIDS Memorial
Atlantic Boulevard & White Street Pier | http://keywestaids.org

If you find yourself at Higgs Beach one afternoon, take a few moments to wander down to the entrance of the White Street Pier off Atlantic Avenue. It's there that you'll find the beautiful Key West AIDS Memorial, the Zimbabwe granite monument that includes the names of those men and women who have died of AIDS and who have shown a love of the Florida Keys by living, working, or visiting here. The peaceful tropical setting provides a quiet place for visitors to express their grief and to reflect on loved ones they themselves may have lost.

NO. 49

Surround yourself with colorful wings at the Key West Butterfly & Nature Conservatory

Key West Butterfly & Nature Conservatory
1316 Duval Street | www.keywestbutterfly.com

Step inside the 5,000-square-foot, glass-domed tropical butterfly habitat and you'll find yourself in a tranquil horticulturists's nirvana. The breathtaking conservatory is a wonderland filled with lush tropical trees and plants with colorful and exotic butterflies fluttering from ceiling to floor. A peaceful stream flows aside a winding path as soft music plays in the background. Hundreds and hundreds of butterflies fly about, feeding from flowers and fresh fruit. If you're lucky, one may even try to land on your shoulder! As you're walking along the trails, you should also be on the lookout for tiny brightly colored songbirds, turtles, and flamingos which also call the conservatory home.

No. 50

Enjoy the island's best conch fritters from the little stand tucked away near the aquarium

Key West Conch Fritters
400 Wall Street (outside the aquarium)

Key West is known for its conch fritters, and the best of this bite-sized snack is found coming from the little pink shack just outside of the aquarium. The fritters (deep-fried balls of sweet conch meat, batter, and seasoning) are all made-to-order and served piping hot, so be patient. And don't miss grabbing some of the Curry family's wonderful Key lime mustard for dipping. For a real treat, order the captain's platter: conch fritters, coconut shrimp, and calamari. It's enough for two!

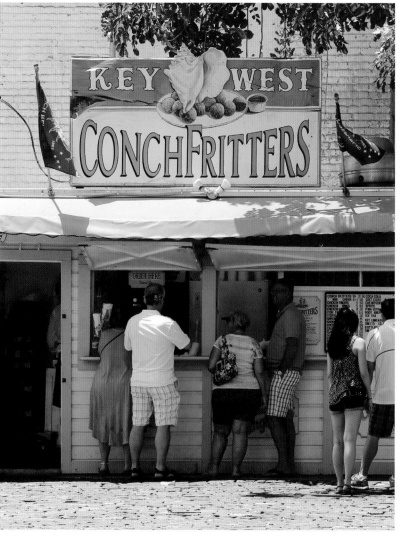

No. 51

Sample more than one hundred hot sauces at the tasting bar at Peppers of Key West

Peppers of Key West
602 Greene Street | www.peppersofkeywest.com

Be prepared to let your taste buds sizzle! Peppers of Key West is stocked wall-to-wall with more than a thousand flavors of hot sauces from around the world, with various degrees of heat ranging from mild to brutally spicy. Hot sauce, barbecue sauce, salsa, jerk sauces, and marinades abound. They even have a glass case filled with ultra-rare limited edition sauces. Belly-up to their tasting bar that's colorfully lined with more than 120 different tiny bottles of sauces ready to be sampled.

TIP: The shop doesn't sell beverages, so if you're going to sample, bring your own beer!

No. 52

Sound the bell for some four-alarm fun at the Key West Firehouse Museum

Key West Firehouse Museum
1026 Grinnell Street | www.keywestfirehousemuseum.com

This small, two-story firehouse at the corner of Grinnell and Virginia Streets is one of the oldest fire stations in Florida. Built in 1907, Fire Station No. 3 has been out of operation since 1998 and now serves as a nifty little firehouse museum. Curated by local historian and retired firefighter Alex Vega, the building houses many interesting artifacts, like an intriguing fire alarm that sent signals through a ticker tape; the only known indoor coal pit; and historic fire helmets, uniforms, and badges. The old living and sleeping quarters have been well-preserved on the second floor. The whole thing wouldn't be complete without the shiny-red, antique, 1929 American La France fire engine. Now go ring that bell!

No. 53

Sip on a tropical cocktail on the popular Sunset Pier as the sun fades below the horizon

Sunset Pier
Behind the Ocean Key Resort | www.oceankey.com/key-west-sunset-pier.aspx

You might think of the famous Sunset Celebration on Mallory Dock as the only place to watch Key West's brilliant sunset. Well, you'd be wrong! The spot that is becoming more and more popular is right next door behind the Ocean Key Resort. The Sunset Pier, comprised of a long wooden dock filled with umbrella tables, nicely positioned stools along the viewing railing, a small bandstand, and what used to be a cute tiki bar (the little round bar has since been remodeled and now resembles a pagoda) is the alternative place to sit, relax, drink, eat, and watch the day come to a spectacular conclusion.

TIP: There's a little-known path on the far front right of Mallory Dock connecting it to the pier. Use it!

No. 54

Watch the colorful handmade ceramics being created at Key West Pottery

Key West Pottery
1203 Duval Street | www.keywestpottery.com

Poke your head into the small doorway at 1203 Duval Street, and you'll be overtaken by a riot of vibrant tropical colors—screaming oranges, sunny yellows, decadent Key lime greens, and riparian blues. You've just entered the creative world of Adam Russell and Kelly Lever, the husband and wife team behind Key West Pottery. Specializing in award-winning contemporary ceramic artworks and functional pottery, their marvelous boutique gallery is filled with ceramic vases, sensational table fish, gorgeous serving bowls, morning coffee mugs, fanciful lidded jars, decorative dinner plates, and magnificent yard sculptures. And you'll probably find one of the friendly, hospitable owners in the tiny workspace in front of the window. Look . . . another masterpiece!

No. 55

Go for an exciting late-afternoon stroll up and down Duval Street

Duval Street
From the Gulf of Mexico to the Atlantic Ocean! | www.duvalstreet.net

Yes, there are many wonderful sights and attractions in Key West, but the one that is almost impossible not to partake in is the stroll down infamous Duval Street, the prominent "main drag" on the island. The downtown, commercially zoned street runs north and south, from the Gulf of Mexico to the Atlantic Ocean. With a carnival-like atmosphere, both sides of the 1.25-mile route are lined with the island's most notorious bars and nightclubs, restaurants, gift shops, tattoo parlors, open-air markets, clothing stores, and miscellaneous tourist attractions.

TIP: Pick up a drink in a plastic cup anywhere you please and feel free to move on—open containers are legal in Key West!

Photo courtesy of Crystal Villegas

No. 56

Take a thrilling kiteboarding lesson and learn to harness the power of the wind

The KiteHouse
1801 North Roosevelt Boulevard | www.thekitehouse.com

Looking for a new adventure while on vacation? Then try kiteboarding lessons with the KiteHouse and master instructor Paul Menta. Paul, a professional kiteboarder who has been teaching the sport since 1999, will show you how to use a large steerable kite to fly around on top of the water while standing on a miniature surfboard. What an exhilarating way to spend an afternoon! His KiteHouse offers classes for beginners, and advanced classes where Paul teaches you his award-winning techniques for doing complex jumps, flips, and other tricks out over the water.

NO. 57

Have a ton of fun out on the ocean on a lively Key West booze cruise

Commotion on the Ocean
Fury Water Adventures | www.furykeywest.com

There's a commotion out on the ocean, and you're invited! You've come to Key West to party, so why not do it in style on Fury Water Adventures' infamous all-you-can-drink sunset sail. The forecast calls for lots of action and good times on the three fun-filled decks of the luxurious state-of-the-art catamaran. The lower deck is where you'll find unlimited food and an open bar, the middle deck has the rockin' dance floor with live bands, and the upper deck is a great place for mingling and meeting new friends. What a fantastic way to party down as the fiery ball sinks into the horizon!

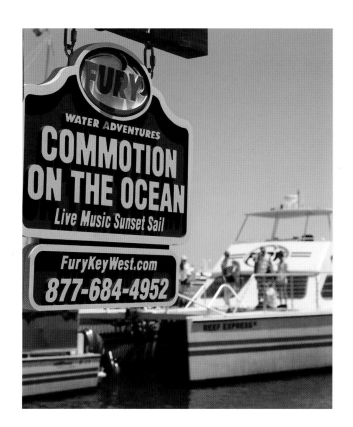

89

Sip & Sail Sunset Cruise
Sunset Watersports Key West
www.sunsetwatersportskeywest.com

Another great choice for unlimited cocktails while sailing into the amazing Key West sunset would be the Sip & Sail cruise offered by Sunset Watersports. The atmosphere aboard their magnificent catamaran is a bit more sedate, with local musicians playing relaxing calypso or reggae music. They also have a very friendly staff that will keep those beverage cups filled and the hors d'oeuvre trays full. Sunset Watersports Key West also offers snorkeling trips, parasailing rides, jet ski tours, and a popular sunset dinner cruise. All in all, the Sip & Sail is a great way to unwind on the waters of paradise.

NO. 58

See the stars perform at the Waterfront Playhouse, the crown jewel of professional theater in the Keys

Waterfront Playhouse
310 Wall Street
www.waterfrontplayhouse.org

Located just steps away from Key West's famous Sunset Celebration on Mallory Square, the intimate 150-seat Waterfront Playhouse is the island's proud community theater. Originally an icehouse in the 1880s, the not-for-profit professional theater now has a nice modern feel that's complemented by a very welcoming staff. The lovely playhouse has been entertaining locals and visitors alike for more than seventy-five years. Its performance season of musicals, comedies, and dramas runs from November through April.

OPPOSITE The Waterfront Playhouse production of Monty Python's *Spamalot*

Photo by Larry Blackbum, provided courtesy of Waterfront Playhouse

Photos courtesy of Nomadic SUP

No. 59

Learn how to paddleboard and then take a tour with Nomadic SUP

Nomadic SUP
Stand Up Paddleboard Tours | www.nomadicsup.com

What an enjoyable and peaceful way to spend time on the water! Cody White, along with his partner Ryan Saca, have created Nomadic SUP (an acronym for Stand Up Paddleboard) in Key West, and they'll not only teach you the techniques and show you how to get comfortable on a paddleboard, but they have formulated a series of tours exclusively for paddleboarders. Cody, a professional paddleboard racer and coach, will guide you on his popular three-hour eco-tour or his sunset paddleboard tour. He also offers private tours (think special occasion) and a natural tour . . . yes, a clothing-optional paddleboard tour. Only in Key West, kids, only in Key West!

No. 60

Buy a fresh coconut from a street cart and enjoy fresh tropical coconut juice!

Coconut Water – as fresh as it gets!
Along Whitehead Street

Nothing beats fresh coconut water (also referred to as coconut juice) right from the nut! So if you're in Key West and want to experience this treat, look for one of the coconut carts that are usually strategically parked around the major tourist attractions like the Hemingway House, the Southernmost Point, or Sunset Celebration. All it takes is a fresh green coco, a few well-placed strikes from a machete or a hole made by a drill, and a nice long straw.

TIP: Plain coconut water is a great cure for a hangover, so start chugging!

No. 61

Visit the eerie East Martello Museum and ask Robert the Haunted Doll for his permission to photograph!

Fort East Martello Museum – Robert the Doll
3501 South Roosevelt Boulevard | www.kwahs.org/museums/fort-east-martello/history

Housed in an 1862 Civil War-era brick fortress overlooking the Atlantic Ocean, East Martello is part historical museum and part Key West gallery. The eight-foot-thick walls surround pictures, artifacts, and historical documents that are intermixed with relics from the Civil War, items from Key West's cigar manufacturing past, and imaginative metal sculptures created by folk artist Stanley Papio. All great stuff of course, but the highlight of any visit is the internationally renowned Robert the Haunted Doll.

Robert the Doll

The most haunted plaything in the world! Dressed in his little sailor suit and clutching a stuffed lion, Robert was known for creating havoc for his original owner Gene Otto. The famous doll is rumored to be haunted, and is said to be the inspiration for the evil character doll "Chucky." Today, Robert is known for casting curses on those who take his photo without first asking permission! And you better ask nicely!

No. 62

Experience the music, drinks, and atmosphere at the world-famous Sloppy Joe's Bar

Sloppy Joe's Bar
201 Duval Street
https://sloppyjoes.com

Not many places say "Key West" more than the iconic Sloppy Joe's Bar. This famous watering hole on the corner of Greene and Duval is ground zero for many a tourist. Often raucous and always rockin', the bar, with its jalousie doors open to the bustling crowd on Duval Street and walls filled with historic pictures and memorabilia, is known worldwide as "the place where Hemingway drank." Fantastic live bands fill the legendary stage from early afternoon until well into the night. And do not leave Key West until you have stopped into Sloppy Joe's gift shop for one of their notorious t-shirts!

No. 63

Follow the trails at the Key West Wildlife Center and get an up close view of the birds and animals

Key West Wildlife Center
1801 White Street | www.keywestwildlifecenter.org

I've been to many wildlife centers before, sometimes only getting a glimpse of just a few wild critters. Not here! This seven-acre designated wildlife refuge is not only heavily populated with creatures, but there are also two large aviaries displaying wild birds whose injuries prevent their release back into nature. Shady paths wind through exotic indigenous plants and trees. Broad-winged hawks, scarlet tanagers, white-crowned pigeons, and American kestrels abound. The center is free, but donations are greatly appreciated.

TIP: Be sure to follow the path all the way back to a neat freshwater pond where white ibises, green iguanas, turtles, tree frogs, and white herons flourish in their natural habitat.

No. 64

Grab a towel and a camera and join Captain Gary on an unforgettable Dolphin Safari

Dolphin Safari
2319 North Roosevelt Boulevard
Banana Bay Resort & Marina | http://safaricharters.com

This exhilarating safari just may be the highlight of your Key West visit! Departing from the Banana Bay Resort Marina on one of the fleet's small speedy boats (holding only six people max), the voyage is an unforgettable three-for-one water adventure. First, Captain Gary will get you to where the dolphins are playing. He's an expert on the tendencies of these marine mammals, knowing them so well he's even given some of them names! The dolphins come so close you could almost reach out and touch them. You're then treated to a marvelous snorkeling adventure, and finally a gentle ride to dry off and watch the amazing Key West sunset. What a beautiful afternoon!

No. 65

Ship home a colorful art original from the tiny David Scott Meier Studio & Gallery

David Scott Meier Studio & Gallery
316 Simonton Street | www.davidscottmeier.com

If you would like to take home a wonderful piece of local artwork, you should stop into the studio of David Scott Meier. David is an exceptional local artist whose colorful textures and designs are intermixed with a marvelous sense of humor. His tiny studio is filled from floor to ceiling with his brilliant oil/mixed media originals and high-quality reproductions. David is best-known for his acclaimed *NICE HAT!* portraits and his popular dog prints, which are decorated with twenty-three carat gold. David is in his studio five days a week. Mondays he goes shopping. Tuesdays he does laundry.

No. 66

Increase your flexibility and
improve your emotional well-being
by attending Yoga on the Beach

Yoga on the Beach
Fort Zachary Taylor State Park | http://yogaonbeach.com

You may never want to practice yoga in any other location again! If you're in Key West and looking to harmonize your mind and body, look no further than Yoga on the Beach. Their giant, canvas yoga mat gets set up right on the sand in front of the beautiful blue Atlantic Ocean in scenic Fort Zachary State Park. Settle into a pose with the gentle sound of the morning waves rolling onto the shore, the cool ocean breeze blowing across the sand, and the rays of the new day's sun peaking through the Australian pines. How awesome is that?

No. 67

Take a self-guided tour of the Curry Inn, one of the most beautiful houses on the island

Amsterdam's Curry Mansion Inn
511 Caroline Street | www.currymansion.com

Built in 1869 by William Curry, reconstructed in 1905 by Milton Curry (Florida's first homegrown millionaire), then restored by Edith and Al Amsterdam in 1975, this magnificent three-story Victorian structure just off Duval Street is part home, part bed and breakfast, and part museum. Feel free to walk through the front door and take a self-guided tour of the public rooms which display an extraordinary selection of antiques and memorabilia. Poke around in the attic and you'll find an 1899 billiard table among the old dresses and luggage.

TIP: Venture up to the widow's walk (built so seamen's wives could watch for the safe return of their husbands' ships) for a marvelous panoramic view of Key West Harbor.

No. 68

Hike along Key West's Historic Seaport and Harbor Walk

Historic Seaport and Harbor Walk
Beginning at the end of Front Street | www.keywesthistoricseaport.com

What years ago was considered a "seedy" part of the island, the redeveloped Key West Seaport and Harbor Walk is now a "do-not-miss" destination in the Conch Republic. This beautiful, scenic two-mile stretch of red bricks and wooden planks winding along the harbor is packed with classic tall ships, catamarans, deep-sea fishing charters, sailboats, and million-dollar yachts on one side and open-air restaurants, trendy gift shops, clothing stores, raw bars, and lively musical entertainment on the other.

TIP: Visit in late afternoon when the deep sea charters return, and watch a lively feeding of the huge tarpons!

No. 69

Dance and party the night away at Bourbon Street Pub, Key West's famously popular gay bar

Bourbon Street Pub
724 Duval Street | www.bourbonstpub.com

With its prime location on Duval Street near the corner of Petronia, the Bourbon Street Pub is the largest and most popular gay nightclub in Key West. The club has something for everyone—special theme nights, live shows, an outdoor patio with a pool, dance music, go-go boys, karaoke, and five bars serving very strong cocktails! The club is always packed until 4 A.M. in the morning, but it's the large bar in front of big opened windows that make Bourbon Pub a great stop in the afternoon (for both people watching and the two-for-one beverages). Talk about a great place to let your hair down . . . this is it!

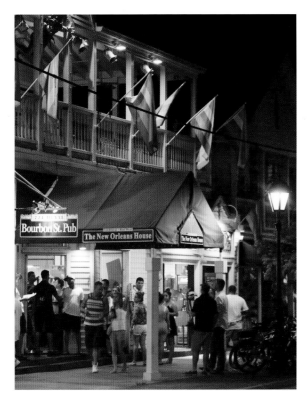

Garden Bar & Pool | Behind Bourbon Street Pub

Not all the action at the Bourbon Street Pub is on the inside. Follow the narrow hallway next to the dance floor and you'll end up outside in the club's wildly popular garden bar and pool area. Belly up to the famed tiki bar for a cold beverage and a chat with the friendly bartenders, or jump in the pool and join the locals in a spirited game of volleyball. You can also relax in their jacuzzi, stretch out on the sun deck, grab a bite to eat from Hazel at the small snack bar, or just people watch from the second-floor viewing deck. There's also a small theater with a stage for live shows during special events. Stop in and say hello to T.J.!

107

No. 70

Tour the Ernest Hemingway
Home & Museum and play with
all the graceful six-toed cats!

Ernest Hemingway Home & Museum
907 Whitehead Street | www.hemingwayhome.com

The Ernest Hemingway Home & Museum is quite possibly the most acclaimed attraction on the island. It was in this very house where the famed author, from his poolside office, wrote several of his most famous books. The home was built by wrecker Ava Tift in 1851, and was extensively remodeled by Ernest and his wife Pauline, who resided here from 1931–1939. Some of the family's actual furnishings are on display, along with memorabilia, photographs, paintings, and first editions of Hemingway's works. The place is usually very crowded with international tourists and descendants of Hemingway's beloved and famed six-toed cats!

TIP: Check out the museum's wonderful new app, viewable at hemingwayhomeapp.com.

No. 71

Enjoy a peaceful walk through the lush, colorful foliage at the Key West Garden Club

Key West Garden Club
1100 Atlantic Boulevard at Higgs Beach | www.keywestgardenclub.com

The Key West Garden Club maintains the lush gardens that flourish inside the West Martello Tower, a historic Civil War-era fort that never really was involved in the war but was instead used for target practice by the U.S. Navy. Enter through the bricked arches, and then stroll a winding series of secluded pathways that reveal a rare collection of native and exotic trees and plants. Among the assortment are blooming orchids, cacti, colorful hibiscus bushes, wondrous strangler fig trees, giant banyan trees, and a Key lime tree. Follow the mysterious trails that lead up to the top of the small hill for a sweeping view of the beautiful Atlantic Ocean.

No. 72

Touch a shark by its tail and get an up close view of the marine animals at the Key West Aquarium

Key West Aquarium
1 Whitehead Street | www.keywestaquarium.com

When the Key West Aquarium opened during the Great Depression in 1934, it was the island's first tourist attraction. It's rather small in size, but it is packed with interesting marine creatures and exhibits. There's a touch tank where you can get close to starfish and sea cucumbers, a stingray exhibit, pools filled with sea turtles and nurse sharks, and tanks with giant moray eels and jellyfish.

TIP: You won't want to miss the shark feedings, which are followed by an opportunity for everyone to touch a shark!

NO. 73

Have your picture taken in front of the famous Mile Marker 0 sign

**The famous Mile Marker 0
Corner of Whitehead & Fleming
Streets**

I wish I had a dime for every time someone asked me where this famous sign is located! Believe it or not, the official green-and-white Mile Marker 0 sign is one of the top attractions on the island. Every day, hundreds, if not thousands of visitors smile for the camera next to this iconic signboard marking the end (or the beginning!) of U.S. 1, the mega-long highway that finds its other end 2,369 miles away in upper Maine. BTW . . . if you're looking for the marker, it's located at the end of U.S. 1!

No. 74

Rent your own jet ski or join a Fury Water Adventures guided jet ski tour

Fury Water Adventures
3841 North Roosevelt Boulevard (at Marriot Beachside) | www.furykeywest.com

Now this is the way to see Key West! You can go it on your own and rent a jet ski from the little tiki hut behind the Marriot Beachside, or join Fury Water Adventures on a guided, twenty-eight-mile tour that circles, weaves, and bobs around the island. You really don't need any experience; the friendly crew will show you everything you need to know to operate the watercraft safely. You'll be flying over the top of the ocean's waves in no time!

TIP: Bring a camera. The tour stops at a desolate sand bar where there is an excellent photo op.

No. 75

Indulge in the decadent treats at Better Than Sex, the island's "must do" desserts-only restaurant

Better Than Sex
926 Simonton Street
www.betterthansexkeywest.com

You better prepare yourself. You're about to enter a dimly lit "bordello" and put some of the most delicious and decadent designer treats you may ever taste in your mouth! Romantic, cozy (tables only sit up to four diners), and extremely popular, the "desserts-only" restaurant's menu features made-on-premises delights with provocative names like Fork-You Fondue (liquid vanilla cheesecake fondue served with donut holes rolled in cinnamon for dipping) and the Missionary Crisp (red apples smothered in a buttery cake-like layer with vanilla ice cream and caramel). The place is always packed, so reservations are an absolute must!

Cookie Nookie Pie

One of many delectable delights featured on the regular menu at Better Than Sex is the Cookie Nookie Pie. Imagine a warm chocolate chip cookie mixed with pecans oozing inside a decadent flaky pie crust, and lying comfortably next to a scoop of vanilla bean ice cream. It's like they were meant to be together! Cover them with freshly whipped crème, drizzles of chocolate and caramel sauce, and a piece of toffee, and you've got a dessert lover's dream!

No. 76

Wait until the sun sets, then take the scary Ghosts & Gravestones Frightseeing Tour

Ghosts & Gravestones Frightseeing Tour
501 Front Street | www.ghostsandgravestones.com

"Yes, we are the doomed!" Walk down any street after dark in Key West and you're bound to hear this chant bellowing from the familiar black trolley as it rolls to its next haunted destination. Narrated by a spooky, costumed, lantern-bearing (albeit friendly) guide, the ninety-minute tour gives you an up close look at all the island's spookier spots, complete with scary, hair-raising tales of murder, disease, and misfortune. The highlight of the tour is the stop at the East Martello Museum and a private encounter with Robert, the world-famous haunted doll (No. 61).

Explore the Tennessee Williams Exhibit honoring the esteemed American playwright's life and works

Tennessee Williams Key West Exhibit
513 Truman Avenue | http://twkw.org

For any fan of American literature, this wonderful collection dedicated to the life and literary accomplishments of one of the foremost playwrights in twentieth-century drama is a must see. Located in a space that is reached by passing through the Key West Business Guild, the exhibit contains first-edition plays, movie posters, rare newspaper and magazine articles, videos, and lots of photographs of his time spent in Key West. Tennessee often visited and eventually lived on the island from 1941 until his death in 1983.

NO. 78

Dip your toes into the water at tiny Simonton Street Beach

Simonton Street Beach
End of Simonton on the Gulf side

You know I like to feature "secret" spots usually only known to the locals. Well, this tiny plot of sand just steps from Duval Street might just be the crown jewel of little-known destinations! What used to be called "Bum Beach" has been remarkably, and I mean remarkably, revamped. This is the only public beach on the island that overlooks the Gulf of Mexico rather than the Atlantic Ocean, and if you are only in town for a couple of days and can't make it out to one of the larger beaches, this is the ideal place to dip your toes in the water! Hidden behind a small parking lot and wedged between the Pier House and Hyatt Resorts, the extremely clean beach is serviced by Lagerheads, a fantastic little beach bar. Make the beach a "must-go" when in Key West!

No. 79

Dig into a legendary cracked conch sandwich at B.O.'s Fish Wagon

B.O.'s Fish Wagon
801 Caroline Street | www.bosfishwagon.com

It looks like a deserted driftwood shack, but B.O.'s Fish Wagon makes some of the best fish sandwiches found on the island. Their cracked conch sandwich served with Key lime mayo is as good as it gets. The rest of the menu here is rather simple—fried fish, burgers, conch fritters, etc.—but the quantity, quality, and freshness of the food is unparalleled. Order at the open-air counter and then take a table surrounded by fishnets, old rusty license plates, lobster traps, old buoys, and roaming chickens. Wash everything down with a couple of cold beers or their refreshing homemade limeade (lemonade made with Key limes). Absolutely delicious!

No. 80

Learn about the plight of South Florida's sea turtles at the Key West Turtle Museum

Key West Turtle Museum
End of Margaret Street in Key West Bight | www.keywestturtlemuseum.org

Wander out on the docks behind the Turtle Kraals Restaurant on Key West's harbor front, and you'll spot a tiny shack that once housed a turtle meat cannery. That weather-worn shanty is now home to the Key West Turtle Museum, devoted to telling the story of how sea turtles were nearly driven to the brink of extinction, and dedicated to the conservation of the turtles, which continue to be threatened with extinction. There are lots of well-organized exhibits, photographs, and displays, and the friendly curator is extremely informative!

No. 81

Encounter the people who have had the greatest impact on Key West at the Memorial Sculpture Garden

Memorial Sculpture Garden
401 Wall Street | www.keywestsculpturegarden.org

Located directly in front of the Waterfront Playhouse in Mallory Square, the Memorial Sculpture Garden proudly displays thirty-six magnificently cast bronze busts, each complete with an extremely informative plaque, of the men and women who have had the greatest impact and influence on this remarkable paradise island. It's a great spot to learn the history and read the stories of influential citizens, local heroes, and famous residents such as railroad tycoon Henry Flagler, U.S. President Harry S. Truman, and famous author Ernest Hemingway.

No. 82

Fill your table with delectable tapas-style small plates at Santiago's Bodega

Santiago's Bodega
207 Petronia Street | www.santiagosbodega.com

One of the more popular restaurants with locals here in Key West is Santiago's Bodega. Located off the beaten path at the far end of Bahama Village, their menu features an excellent selection of both hot and cold "tapas-style" plates influenced by the cuisines of Spain, Greece, and the Mediterranean. You can dine inside or you can sit outdoors along the small side street and share small plates like yellow fin ceviche, skewered shrimp and chorizo, bacon and basil stuffed mushrooms, or warm dates stuffed with goat cheese. And wash it all down with their delicious homemade sangria. Paradise found, yet again!

No. 83

Drop in to the country's only jailhouse petting zoo, the Monroe County Sheriff's Animal Farm

Monroe County Sheriff's Animal Farm
5501 College Road, Stock Island | www.keysso.net/miscellaneous/animal_park.htm

What an extremely unique way to see and interact with animals! The Sheriff's Animal Farm, lovingly managed by friendly and informative farmer Jeanne Salander, sprawls out beneath the jail which was built on stilts eleven feet above ground. The farm, which started out as a haven for ducks and roosters injured in traffic, now houses more than 150 abused and abandoned animals such as alpacas, giant tortoises, exotic lizards, tropical birds, and a very engaging sloth! The sheriff's farm is open to the public on the second and fourth Sunday of each month. Well done Farmer Jeanne!

No. 84

Board a high-speed catamaran
and explore Fort Jefferson and the
Dry Tortugas National Park

Dry Tortugas National Park Ferry
100 Grinnell Street | www.drytortugas.com

If you love to snorkel or bird watch, don't miss the opportunity to travel the seventy miles beyond Key West to the Dry Tortugas National Park. Hop aboard the *Yankee Freedom* for the two-hour ride over the open water and you'll arrive at the tiny island that is home to Fort Jefferson, America's largest nineteenth-century coastal fort. The island is surrounded by crystal clear waters, superlative coral reefs, and abundant tropical fish, making it a perfect place to enjoy an afternoon of snorkeling. The national park is also especially popular with birders, who come to observe the nearly 300 species of migrating birds that frequent the Dry Tortugas.

No. 85

Do a little sportfishing out on the ocean and return with a boatload of mahi-mahi

Discretion Sportfishing
202 William Street
www.discretionsportfishing.com

If you ever wanted to go big-time sport fishing, you might as well do it right here in the Florida Keys. More saltwater world records have been established here than any other destination on the globe. Jump on any of the professionally guided charters leaving from the historic seaport, and be prepared to haul in swordfish, mahi-mahi, tuna, shark, barracuda, hogfish, snapper, wahoo, marlin, or many of the other species found in the deep-blue Atlantic. You can take a trip anytime, day or night, it's totally at your discretion!

No. 86

Shop Mallory Square and load up on every type of inexpensive souvenir imaginable

Mallory Square Shopping
400 Wall Street | www.mallorysquare.com

Historic Mallory Square is generally known for three things. It is home to the fantastic Sunset Celebration, it's an area where you can find many of the island's tourist attractions, and it is *the* place to pick up every type of low-priced memento imaginable. This plaza in Old Town is lined with open-air stores and colorful souvenir carts piled high with loads of inexpensive items like straw hats, t-shirts, seashells, replica alligators, chimes, funny coconuts, flip-flops, and magnets. Tourist central—indeed it is!

TIP: You will also find many shops in the blocks surrounding Mallory Square with storefront barkers yelling, "Everything . . . five dollars!"

Photo courtesy of Southernmost Scavenger Hunt Inc.

No. 87

Team up with Southernmost Scavenger Hunt and follow Pinky's clues all over paradise

Southernmost Scavenger Hunt
631 Greene Street | http://keywesthunt.com

One of the more unusual ways to discover the sites in Key West just might be the Southernmost Scavenger Hunt. Get a few groups of friends together and follow a series of Pinky the Pink Coconut's clues to discover fun facts and interesting trivia while searching famous sites and hidden local hotspots. The hunts are really a great way to explore the nooks and crannies of Old Town; and they make for a really fun outing if you're here for a birthday bash, corporate event, or wedding party.

No. 88

Get a taste of the Caribbean by visiting the colorful neighborhood of Bahama Village

Bahama Village
Centered around 400 Petronia Street

Get a taste of the Caribbean by visiting Key West's Bahama Village, a sixteen-block neighborhood off Whitehead Street featuring quirky souvenir carts, pastel-painted boutiques and art galleries, colorful Conch houses with small yards overflowing with lush vegetation, and fabulous Bahamian-influenced restaurants with lively outdoor bars. Expect plenty of tropical influences in the cuisine—mango, pineapple, jerk, curries, coconut, and plantains. Take your own little walking tour around this pleasant neighborhood and you'll feel as if you've been to the Bahamas!

No. 89

Enjoy the beauty of nature at the Key West Tropical Forest & Botanical Garden

Key West Tropical Forest & Botanical Gardens
5210 College Road, Stock Island | www.kwbgs.org

Maintained by volunteers since 1935, this eleven-acre tropical forest and garden is a wonderful opportunity to view native plants, exotic endangered flora and fauna, and rare tropical palm trees. A series of walking paths are nicely shaded by the canopy; and you'll spot numerous butterflies, iguanas, birds, and turtles in the ponds during your peaceful hike. Unusual plants and beautiful flowers abound.

TIP: If you're a serious birder, follow the rugged trail off Desbiens Pond that leads to a very large pond (not on the map) in the rear of the forest. It's a popular stop for migrating birds!

Rare Palm
Tour
Starts here at Stop #120
Cell Phone Tour dial 305-744-5036, follow instructions.

HODGKINS PUBLIC LIBRARY

No. 90
Try the handcrafted cocktails at Agave 308, the island's popular tequila bar

Agave 308 Tequila Bar
308 Front Street | www.agave308.com

Standing in Mallory Square you will have two great views. Look one way, and you'll see a fabulous sunset. Turn around, and you'll be staring at the best darn margaritas in Key West! Agave 308, located just beneath the Rooftop Café, is the island's first and only tequila bar. Dimly lit and sophisticated, the bar features more than ninety different one hundred percent blue agave tequilas. The bartenders here use fresh lime juice, agave nectar, and pressed herbs to produce an amazing selection of creative, handcrafted cocktails. Very popular with the locals, the bar also offers a small selection of snacks, including gourmet tacos and homemade chips with salsa.

No. 91

Have your hair styled like a rock star at the always entertaining Bobbyshop Hair Salon

Bobbyshop Hair Salon
328 Southard Street | www.bobbyshoponline.com

On vacation and need a great cut? Then follow the locals over to the coolest salon on the island. Owner Bobby Donahue was one of NYC's top stylists, with celebrity clients all over the country, but the warm weather drew him, and his love for '50s pop culture, to Key West. Check out his colorful shop, filled with rock 'n' roll memorabilia and a marvelous staff that shares his vision of entertaining while styling your hair.

TIP: This tip comes directly from Bobby, "For great looking hair, squeeze three limes into a glass and rinse through your hair. Next, squeeze three more limes into a glass and add tequila, sugar, and ice. Mix, drink, and watch the sunset."

No. 92

Check out the period furnishings and antiques inside the Oldest House in South Florida

The Oldest House in Key West
322 Duval Street | www.oirf.org

Easily found on the busier end of Duval Street, this Conch-style cottage was constructed in 1829, making it the oldest known house on the island. It was once the home of Sea Captain Francis Watlington and his family, whose descendants resided here until 1972. Enjoy the free admission (donations accepted) and check out original furnishings, family portraits, model ships, and historical documents. Amazingly, the house has survived fires, hurricanes, economic hardships, the occupation of Union troops, and, more recently, lines of sightseeing tourists!

No. 93

Sip away at a free tasting of unusual, tropical fruit wines at Key West Winery

Key West Winery
103 Simonton Street | www.thekeywestwinery.com

Wine without grapes? You bet! Key West Winery specializes in a line of super premium tropical fruit wines using fruits, berries, and citrus. Stop into their colorful shop and tasting room on Simonton Street and try their unusual, full-bodied, flavorful wines with fun little names like Mango Momma, Florida Sunset Pineapple, King Kiwi, and Hurricane White Sangria. You could grab a few bottles to take home or Key West Winery will be glad to ship them for you.

TIP: If you're with the kids, exit out the rear. There's a giant alligator statue that makes for an excellent photo op!

No. 94

Feel your heart pound while parasailing high above the Atlantic Ocean

Parasailing with Sebago Watersports
205 Elizabeth Street | www.keywestsebago.com

Are you secretly hiding a little thrill-seeker inside you? Then it's time to let it all hang out by soaring way, way up there out over the wondrous aqua-blue Atlantic Ocean on a breathtaking parasailing adventure. Strap on a harness and you'll get a bird's-eye view from more than 300 feet above the water while hanging from Sebago Watersports's recognizable red, orange, yellow, and blue parasail. You can chose to have your one-hour adventure mild and dry or wet and wild. In either case, get ready to feel like Superman!

Photo Courtesy of Mary Veal Photography

No. 95

Grab a good book and lay out at Smathers Beach, the largest public beach on the island

Smathers Beach
South Roosevelt Boulevard | www.keywesttravelguide.com/smathers-beach

If you find yourself in need of some uninterrupted peace and quiet, grab a book and head over to Smathers Beach, the largest stretch of sand on the island. The beach does have its good points and its bad points. The good: the shear length of the beach allows for long walks along the water and lots of room to find your own private space. It's also very scenic, with swaying palm trees lined up as far as the eye can see and kite boarders surfing the waves off in the distance. The beach has volleyball nets, cold showers, kayak and raft rentals, and a nice line of food trucks along Roosevelt Boulevard. The bad: it's just not very good for swimming. The water is not very deep and usually filled with seaweed. But it is very scenic!

No. 96

Savor the yummy flavors of
tropical homemade ice cream
at Flamingo Crossing

Flamingo Crossing Ice Cream
1105 Duval Street | 305-296-6124

There are a number of shops with decent ice cream in Old Town, but the cream of the crop is Flamingo Crossing. Located down Duval Street, closer to the Southernmost Point than Mallory Square, this tiny converted shotgun house dishes out the most flavorful, tropically flavored homemade gelatos you might ever have the pleasure of tasting. The interior is stark and the line is known for moving rather slow, but when you've tasted their flavors like Tahitian vanilla, Cuban coffee, papaya, guanabana, Key lime, and raspberry cappuccino, you'll be glad you stopped.

No. 97

Savor the Godiva White Chocolate French Toast at Camille's, a funky local favorite!

Camille's Restaurant
1202 Simonton Street | www.camilleskeywest.com

There are many fabulous places with great breakfast items on their menu, but the locals here flock to the one with the bright pink façade on Simonton Street. The funky restaurant with the kitschy décor has been around for more than twenty years, and they are as well-known for their colorful quirky knickknacks that fill the walls and shelves as they are for their food. Order up their Godiva White Chocolate French Toast, and then check out the Barbie doll collection and the signature statue of the two pigs "makin' bacon." If you sleep in past three, they also serve lunch and dinner!

No. 98

See how that sweet libation is made at the Key West First Legal Rum Distillery

Key West First Legal Rum Distillery
105 Simonton Street | www.keywestlegalrum.com

The old Coca-Cola bottling plant on Simonton Street is now where you'll find the First Legal Rum Distillery. Take the short tour in Paul Menta's rum factory, decoratively filled with aging barrels and fermentation tanks, and you'll learn all about the history of rum making, from the legal to the illegal! Afterwards, there's a nice little free rum tasting in the reception area.

TIP: For a small fee you can upgrade to the popular flight tasting and try Paul's creatively flavored rums like Vanilla Brulee Dark, Mojito Mint, and Glazed Pineapple.

No. 99

Grab one of the best breakfasts in town at rustic Pepe's Café, another local favorite!

Pepe's Café
806 Caroline Street | www.pepeskeywest.com

Every time I return to Key West, I try to stop into Pepe's at least once. This popular place is a true Key West landmark, and it really makes you feel as if you are dining in the authentic Old Town Key West. And it should, as Pepe's was established in 1909, making it the oldest eatery in the Florida Keys. The cafe does serve lunch and dinner, but it's the breakfast here that I love. Classic omelets or pancakes along with fresh-squeezed orange juice and a hot coffee in the charming outdoor garden is the way to begin any day!

TIP: If you can't get a table, there's a neat little bar in the back corner of the patio that just might have an empty seat or two!

No. 100

Enjoy a romantic picnic lunch on Fort Zachary Taylor State Park Beach

Fort Zachary Taylor State Park Beach
Southern tip of Key West | https://www.floridastateparks.org/park/Fort-Taylor

As any local will tell you, this is by far the nicest beach on the island. The water is deep and clear, the sand is soft and well-maintained, and it's likely you'll be able to spot many colorful tropical fish near the limestone breakwater. You might come to "Fort Zach" to swim, snorkel, sunbathe, bike, or fish, but do pack a lunch. The beach is scattered with picnic tables and barbecue grills, and the lofty Australian pine trees provide plenty of shade. It's a perfect place for a nice little romantic feast!

TIP: The beach also offers one of the best, unobstructed views of the sunset away from the maddening crowds on Mallory Dock or Sunset Pier.

No. 101

Get up early, realize you're on vacation,
and go back to bed!

SWEET DREAMS AND HAPPY TRAVELS!

IOI
THINGS
TO DO

(IN A HANDY LIST)

For your convenience, here's a quick-look reference list of all the ideas in this book. Check off as many as you can each time you return to Key West! And keep in mind, the list is in no particular order. I haven't put the "best" things first; each is wonderful in its own right. Also, some of the activities may be weather-permitting, seasonal, or held at scheduled times, so please check ahead for current updates and availabilities. I hope you get to experience all the wonderful things to do in Key West, and that your visit will be memorable!

1. Start your day with an elegant Morning Mimosa Sail aboard the Schooner *Hindu*

2. Climb to the top of the Key West Lighthouse for a panoramic view of the city

3. Indulge in a little slice of paradise at the original Kermit's Key West Key Lime Pie Shoppe

4. Join the locals in a spirited game of beach volleyball at Higgs Beach

5. Dine above the streets and beneath the stars at the Roof Top Café, a local favorite!

6. Get an up close look at the sharks with Key West Extreme Adventures Shark Tours

7. Have your photo taken standing next to the colorful buoy at the Southernmost Point

8. Head over to Sand-Isle and take a professionally taught sand sculpting class

9. Win some really wild prizes at the multi-decade island tradition of Drag Queen Bingo

10. Join the crowds on Mallory Dock for the nightly Sunset Celebration

11. Combine a sophisticated drink with some great tunes at the Little Room Jazz Club

12. Warm your spirit with a selection of fine rums at the historic Speakeasy Inn Rum Bar

13. Discover splendid local artwork and historical artifacts at the Key West Museum of Art & History

14. Get a load of all the colorfully dressed characters masquerading around the island!

15. Experience a historic presidential winter retreat at the Harry S. Truman Little White House

16. Jump on the Old Town Trolley and be treated to a narrated tour of the island

17. Peddle through hidden back streets and sample local fruits on Lloyd's Tropical Bike Tour

18. Interact with the rescued orphaned parrots and macaws at Nancy Forrester's Secret Garden

19. Savor an authentic Cuban café con leche at the popular Sandy's Café

20. Pick up some exotic seashells at the Shell Warehouse

21. Stumble down the alley to Virgilio's Martini Madness Monday

22. Travel up to Big Pine Key to get a glimpse of the miniature Key Deer

23. Feast on creative Caribbean cuisine served in a tropical paradise at the ultra-funky Blue Heaven

24. Say a little prayer amongst the architectural beauty of The Basilica of Saint Mary Star of the Sea

25. Marvel at fragrant orchids and rare tropical palms at the Audubon House & Tropical Gardens

26. Kick back on an unforgettable sunset cruise and sail into Key West's remarkable sunset

27. Climb aboard the Conch Tour Train and learn all about the history of Key West

28. Slip on a handmade pair of sandals at the world-famous Kino Sandals Factory

29. Party the night away at the Green Parrot, a popular dive bar featuring great local live music

30. Jump on a Perfect Pedicab and be blissfully peddled to your next destination

31. Spend the day with nature paddling around the scenic mangroves

32. Belly up to the bar at Schooner Wharf and enjoy a cold beer and great live music

33. Discover the "era of the wreckers" at the Key West Shipwreck Museum

34. Take in a legendary drag performance at the iconic La Te Da Cabaret

35. Take the self-guided tour of the huge Civil War-era Fort Zachary Taylor

36. Enjoy a nice hand-rolled Cuban leaf cigar

37. Follow the aroma into Old Town Bakery and get your hands on their delicious sticky buns

38. Relax by one of the three outdoor pools at the affordable Southwinds Motel

39. Step aboard a U.S. battleship at the USCGC *Ingham* Maritime Museum

40. Take in a foreign or indie film at the intimate Tropic Cinema

41. Dig into the most authentic Cuban home cooking in Florida at El Siboney Restaurant

42. Reserve a poolside room or just visit and join the fun at the Island House Resort

43. Rejuvenate your mind, body, and spirit with a massage on the beach at Spa al Mare

44. Join the free walking tour of the aboveground vaults in historic Key West Cemetery

45. Slip on your fins and go snorkeling in the world-famous Florida Keys Coral Reef

46. Buy the freshest fish on the island at Tomasita Seafood, a "secret" local favorite!

47. Journey into a world of native plants and animals at the Florida Keys Eco-Discovery Center

48. Pay tribute to those who have died of AIDS at the Key West AIDS Memorial

49. Surround yourself with colorful wings at the Key West Butterfly & Nature Conservatory

50. Enjoy the island's best conch fritters from the little stand tucked away near the aquarium

51. Sample more than one hundred hot sauces at the tasting bar at Peppers of Key West

52. Sound the bell for some four-alarm fun at the Key West Firehouse Museum

53. Sip on a tropical cocktail on the popular Sunset Pier as the sun fades below the horizon

54. Watch the colorful handmade ceramics being created at Key West Pottery

55. Go for an exciting late-afternoon stroll up and down Duval Street

56. Take a thrilling kiteboarding lesson and learn to harness the power of the wind

57. Have a ton of fun out on the ocean on a lively Key West booze cruise

58. See the stars perform at the Waterfront Playhouse, the crown jewel of professional theater in the Keys

59. Learn how to paddleboard and then take a tour with Nomadic SUP

60. Buy a fresh coconut from a street cart and enjoy fresh tropical coconut juice!

61. Visit the eerie East Martello Museum and ask Robert the Haunted Doll for his permission to photograph!

62. Experience the music, drinks, and atmosphere at the world-famous Sloppy Joe's Bar

63. Follow the trails at the Key West Wildlife Center and get an up close view of the birds and animals

64. Grab a towel and a camera and join Captain Gary on an unforgettable Dolphin Safari

65. Ship home a colorful art original from the tiny David Scott Meier Studio & Gallery

66. Increase your flexibility and improve your emotional well-being by attending Yoga on the Beach

67. Take a self-guided tour of the Curry Inn, one of the most beautiful houses on the island

68. Hike along Key West's Historic Seaport and Harbor Walk

69. Dance and party the night away at Bourbon Street Pub, Key West's famously popular gay bar

70. Tour the Ernest Hemingway Home & Museum and play with all the graceful six-toed cats!

71. Enjoy a peaceful walk through the lush, colorful foliage at the Key West Garden Club

72. Touch a shark by its tail and get an up close view of the marine animals at the Key West Aquarium

73. Have your picture taken in front of the famous Mile Marker 0 sign

74. Rent your own jet ski or join a Fury Water Adventures guided jet ski tour

75. Indulge in the decadent treats at Better Than Sex, the island's "must do" desserts-only restaurant

76. Wait until the sun sets, then take the scary Ghosts & Gravestones Frightseeing Tour

77. Explore the Tennessee Williams Exhibit honoring the esteemed American playwright's life and works

78. Dip your toes into the water at tiny Simonton Street Beach

79. Dig into a legendary cracked conch sandwich at B.O.'s Fish Wagon

80. Learn about the plight of South Florida's sea turtles at the Key West Turtle Museum

81. Encounter the people who have had the greatest impact on Key West at the Memorial Sculpture Garden

82. Fill your table with delectable tapas-style small plates at Santiago's Bodega

83. Drop in to the country's only jailhouse petting zoo, the Monroe County Sheriff's Animal Farm

84. Board a high-speed catamaran and explore Fort Jefferson and the Dry Tortugas National Park

85. Do a little sportfishing out on the ocean and return with a boatload of mahi-mahi

86. Shop Mallory Square and load up on every type of inexpensive souvenir imaginable

87. Team up with Southernmost Scavenger Hunt and follow Pinky's clues all over paradise

88. Get a taste of the Caribbean by visiting the colorful neighborhood of Bahama Village

89. Enjoy the beauty of nature at the Key West Tropical Forest & Botanical Garden

90. Try the handcrafted cocktails at Agave 308, the island's popular tequila bar

91. Have your hair styled like a rock star at the always entertaining Bobbyshop Hair Salon

92. Check out the period furnishings and antiques inside the Oldest House in South Florida

93. Sip away at a free tasting of unusual, tropical fruit wines at Key West Winery

94. Feel your heart pound while parasailing high above the Atlantic Ocean

95. Grab a good book and lay out at Smathers Beach, the largest public beach on the island

96. Savor the yummy flavors of tropical homemade ice cream at Flamingo Crossing

97. Savor the Godiva White Chocolate French Toast at Camille's, a funky local favorite!

98. See how that sweet libation is made at the Key West First Legal Rum Distillery

99. Grab one of the best breakfasts in town at rustic Pepe's Café, another local favorite!

100. Enjoy a romantic picnic lunch on Fort Zachary Taylor State Park Beach

101. Get up early, realize you're on vacation, and go back to bed!

INDEX

801 Bourbon Bar 27
Agave 308 130
AIDS Memorial 79
Aquarium 110
Audubon House 48
Bahama Village 126-127
Bars & Nightclubs
   801 Bourbon Bar 27
   Agave 308 130
   Bourbon St. Pub 107
   Green Parrot Bar 56-57
   La Te Da 63
   Little Room Jazz Club 32
   Rum Bar 33
   Schooner Wharf 60-61
   Sloppy Joe's 98-99
   Sunset Pier 85
   Virgilio's 44
Basilica of St. Mary 47
Beaches
   Fort Zachary 142
   Higgs Beach 20-21
   Simonton Beach 116
   Smathers Beach 135
Better Than Sex 113
Blue Heaven 46
B.O.'s Fish Wagon 117

Bobbyshop Hair Salon 131
Botanical Garden 128-129
Bourbon Street Pub 107
Brendan Orr 23
Butterfly Conservatory 80-81
Camille's Restaurant 137
Cemetery 75
Cigars 66-67
Coast Guard Museum 70
Commotion on Ocean 89
Conch Fritters 82
Conch Tour Train 54
Contents 3
Curry Inn 105
Customs House 34-35
David Scott Meier 103
Discretion Sportfishing 123
Dolphin Safari 76, 102
Drag Queen Bingo 27
Dry Tortugas Ferry 122
Duval Street 87
East Martello Museum 96-97
Eco-Discovery Center 78
El Siboney Restaurant 72
Ernest Hemingway Home 108
Extreme Shark Tours 24
Firehouse Museum 84
First Legal Rum Distillery 138-139
Flamingo Crossing 136
Fort Zachary Taylor Beach 142
Fort Zachary Taylor St. Park 64-65, 142

Fury Water Adventures
    Commotion Ocean 89
    Jet Ski Tour 112
Garden Club 109
Ghosts & Gravestones 114
Green Parrot Bar 56-57
Handy List 145-149
Harbor Walk 106
Harry S. Truman 38
Higgs Beach 20-21
Hindu, Schooner 7, 16-17
Island House Resort 73, 143
Jet Ski Tour 112
Jonathan Gross 7, 22
Kermit's Key West Key Lime Pie 19
Key Deer 45
Key West Pottery 86
Key West Winery 133
Kino Sandals Factory 55
KiteHouse 88
La Te Da 63
Lands End Sunset Sail 50-51
Lighthouse 18
Lil' Ed & Blues Imperials 57
Little Room Jazz Club 32
Little White House 38
Lloyd's Tropical Bike Tour 40
Mallory Square 28-31, 124
Martini Madness Monday 44
Memorial Sculpture Garden 119

Mile Marker 0 111
Morning Mimosa Cruise 7, 16-17
Museums & Exhibits
    Art & History 34-35
    Curry Inn 105
    East Martello 96-97
    Eco-Discovery Center 78
    Ernest Hemingway 108
    Firehouse 84
    Fort Zachary Taylor 64-65
    Little White House 38
    Oldest House 132
    Sculpture Garden 119
    Shipwreck Treasure 62
    Tennessee Williams 115
    Turtle Museum 118
    USCGC *Ingham* 70
Nancy Forrester's Garden 41
Nomadic SUP 94
Ocean Key Resort 85
Old Town Bakery 68
Old Town Trolley 39
Oldest House 132
Parasailing 134
Paul Menta 138
Pepe's Café 140-141
Peppers 83
Perfect Pedicab 58
Preface 4
Q Mitch 27
Randy Roberts 63

Red Mangrove Kayaking 59
Restaurants
    Better Than Sex 113
    Blue Heaven 46
    B.O.'s Fish Wagon 117
    Camille's 137
    Conch Fritters 82
    El Siboney 72
    Flamingo Crossing 136
    Old Town Bakery 68
    Pepe's Café 140-141
    Rooftop Café 13, 22-23
    Sandy's Café 42
    Santiago's Bodega 120
Robert the Doll 97
Roof Top Café 13, 22-23
Rum Bar 33
Saint Mary's Church 47
Sand-Isle 26
Sandy's Café 42
Santiago's Bodega 120
Schooner *Appledore II* 52-53
Schooner *Hindu* 7, 16-17
Schooner *Wharf Bar* 60-61
Schooner *When & If* 49
Seaport & Harbor Walk 106
Sebago Watersports
    Lands End Sunset Sail 50-51
    Parasailing 134
    Windjammer Sunset Sail 52-53
Shell Warehouse 43

Sheriff's Animal Farm 121
Shipwreck Museum 62
Simonton Beach 116
Sip & Sail Sunset Cruise 90-91
Sloppy Joe's Bar 98-99
Smathers Beach 135
Snorkeling 76
Southernmost Point 25
Southernmost Scavenger Hunt 125
Southwinds Motel 69
Spa al Mare 74
Speakeasy Inn Rum Bar 33
Sunset Celebration 28-31
Sunset Pier 85
Sunset Sail Key West 49
Sunset Watersports 90-91
Tennessee Williams 115
Tomasita Seafood 77
Tropic Cinema 71
Tropical Forest 128-129
Turtle Museum 118
USCGC *Ingham* 70
Virgilio's 44
Waterfront Playhouse 92-93
Wildlife Center 100-101
Windjammer Sunset Sail 52-53
Yankee Freedom 122
Yoga on the Beach 104